*#Maipiùsposebambine* Inquiry
**[No more child brides]**

# I'M ONLY
# A CHILD

*(Stories of abuse and mistreatment
in the denied childhood of child brides)*

Wanda Montanelli

# CHAPTER I

# STORIES ABOUT CHILD BRIDES

*To all the courageous little girls who started
the protest against child marriage,
and all the others who, although forced to marry,
are fighting for a better fate for their own children*

# From dolls to husbands

*These are true stories.*
*They took place in countries where it is customary to oblige young girls to go from playing with dolls to being controlled by a husband, who is often elderly, a stranger, someone chosen by their family.*

## The Tortured Child Bride
## A Symbol of Human Rights

Sahar Gul's story is emblematic and a testimony to unacceptable cruelty.

The image of the little girl who her torturers forced into prostitution is a picture of suffering: her swollen eyes, the bruised skin on her face, a burnt ear, her hands - without nails because the vile criminals pulled them off - are covered in dark scabs and wounds.

Everyone who's seen the photograph of the small victim has felt a surge of revulsion and rebellion. Civil society, the press, social networks, associations, have all made their strong disagreement and condemnation of the child's persecutor heard.

## Sahar Gul refused to be a prostitute and she was massacred

The reason for all this fury was because the little girl refused to be a prostitute. As a little slave, forced into early marriage, she quickly realized there were no limits to the cruelty of her tyrant husband, the soldier Gulam Sakhi. The adult man who, in addition to having violated her innocence, felt he could make money out of her emaciated body, by selling her to his sickening peers.

He claimed powers of life or death over the child and helped by relatives - as cruel and greedy as himself - he made Sahar endure paid sexual encounters, with men of all ages, to make money and profit ruthlessly.

Sahar's and Gulam's is one of the many -too many- forced marriages, which when described truthfully, are nothing more than the actions of paedophiles against innocent little girls.
Right from the start, the intentions of the soldier's entire family unit were to earn money by offering his little wife to sate the appetites of perverts, ignoring the little girl's protests, her pain, her immense disgust.

## An impossible life, then her escape and salvation

What happens in a house where adults hold a minor prisoner? And how does a twelve-year-old girl, caught in the trap, feel?
At first Sahar didn't realise the irreversibility of her state. They told her that getting married was a duty, a natural event, the only way to exist with dignity, with the man of the house responsible for the entire household. They told her this is what women have to do: get married, obey their husband and have children. They forced her to accept marriage, especially her parents, her mother. How she would have loved to have a sympathetic

mother, one she could turn to for help in understanding what was happening to her, how all the other men who claimed her body fitted into the picture: old men, young men, strangers for whom she felt repulsion, who as they got closer to her made her heart seem about to burst from beating so fast, or just stop out of fear.

She hated them. And she hated her husband. She detested all the adults who portrayed marriage as a happy event to her. She found no confirmation of all their promises. She had thought, that although she was being forced to marry, she would find affection, loving gestures, comforting words, nice manners. But there was none of any of this. She was trapped and her husband was a tormentor; neither husband, nor friend, nor relation. A brute. Her mother-in-law and all the rest of the family were even worse than him. And Sahar was only a child.

Sahar didn't know who to turn to among the people who came and went in her home.

She showed signs of distress when she heard her relatives' unbelievable words as they insisted - every time a stranger crossed the threshold - in persuading her to whore. She refused, she screamed, she cried; but her husband and in-laws quickly went from words to more forceful methods: they used threats and any other means of coercion to break down the child's resistance.

It was impossible for Sahar to live with the fear, the sleepless nights, the dread of being insulted and offended every day. The awareness that there would never be either freedom or a future in her life, drove her to react.

One day she ran away and asked the neighbours for help: "They force me to have sex with other men! - she said - If you're Muslims you have to help me and tell the police what they're doing to me."

The neighbours immediately reported what was happening. The police intervened and summoned Gulam Sakhi who, saying he was sorry, promised to end the torture against Sahar. He asked the little girl to return home.

Unfortunately, the police - after giving Gulam a warning - sent Sahar back home, pretending they believed in the man's remorse and his words of repentance.

However, when dealing with an ogre, you have to take into account that it is unforgivably foolish to leave a child in his hands. In no story, be it true or a fairy tale, are ogres transformed into lambs by a simple recommendation from the authorities.

**After returning home the nightmare just got worse for Sahar**

In the little house, a cramped space in the district of Pol-e Khomri in Baghlan province, the worst period began, one of torture for Sahar who, beaten, chained up and left without food, was shut up in a basement. Wounded, insulted, in pain, she was left

to the mercy of her relatives - who behaved like true criminals - until, many months later, one of her uncles went to visit her. The man realised that the child's face was swollen, her whole body covered in bruises, her eyes full of tears. He was astonished. He realised he was faced with inconceivable cruelty.
He immediately decided to report the matter to the police and go public about the disgrace.

He told as many people as possible, as well as the authorities, about the little girl's scandalous treatment, which was comparable to medieval torture; a violence so brutal as to reduce her to using a wheelchair for a long time when she was no longer able to walk.
The picture of the massacred little girl travelled all around the world. Thanks to the interest of the press, Sahar's swollen face, her black eyes, her wounded body, her unhappy gaze, were seen all over Afghanistan, and then through websites, blogs, social pages dealing with human rights, the case became an ultra-national disgrace, despite the authorities and the family trying to conceal the sinister and cruel affair.


**A committee of inquiry set up by the President**

Hamid Karzai, the president of Afghanistan, ordered a committee of inquiry to be set up, following which Sahar's ineffable husband and criminal relatives were prosecuted by law, with the immediate arrest of her relatives and an arrest warrant issued for Gulam Sakhi who went into hiding. However, the judgment was broadcast on Afghan national television and there were not many places where the man could hide. It was the month of May 2012. In July, Sahar's mother-in-law, father-in-law and sister-in-law were sentenced to ten years in prison for attempted murder.

## But how could someone ever have absolute power over a child-wife?

Sahar's story began in May 2011, when she was only 12 years old, and was sold for five thousand dollars to her torturers, who immediately organised a forced marriage whereby they gained all legal power over the child.

The plan was to exploit her sexually and get paid handsomely by nonchalant paedophiles who, confident of her husband's consent, were not moved to pity by Sahar's tears or suffering gaze, and defiled her without any scruples whatsoever.

Sahar Gul's segregation in the home lasted until the day of her uncle's intervention, the police's subsequent action and President Karzai's decision, following the uproar on the pages of authoritative newspapers around the world.

The Times contributed to the dissemination very effectively in its Afghan publications, with articles entitled "Let's break the deathly silence on the status of women".

Newspapers, magazines, blogs, intensified the public debate until the parliamentary institutions approved a law making "domestic violence" a crime.

So there began in the country an acknowledgement and a process of civilisation of a part of society that still considers powers of life or death over wives to be legitimate, even if they are only little girls. But this is only an encouraging start because the outcome of the story leaves a bitter taste in the mouth.

## Ten year prison sentences for the torturers which they don't serve

Although the case created an outcry in international public opinion, after Sahar's three torturers were sentenced to ten years in prison, the Court - during a further hearing in a half-empty courtroom - ordered the release of the three people responsible, in the absence of counterparties and the ministerial authorities.

The Court of Appeals subsequently condemned the torturers to five years, with the possibility for the victim to claim damages.

During the trial, Sahar took refuge with the *Women for Afghan Women* Association, the organisation which takes care of abused Afghan women, offering them legal protection and hospitality in specifically organised shelters.

On International Women's Day in 2012, an Internet café for women was opened in the Afghan capital, Kabul, in the name of Sahar Gul.
What with the acknowledgements of civil society and the feeling of having done the right thing Sahar realised there was a ray of light for her, even if unfortunately, her disappointments were not over. She alternated between moments of hope and others of disappointment. She knew that unfortunately the process in the courts was not complete; she would gladly have done without further ordeals, interrogations, confrontations with those who had wronged her. She suffered in seeing her relatives again, and each time hoped it would be for last time. One day her bitterness was rekindled because a further ruling ordered the release of her torturers.

Sahar nevertheless decided to look to the future. With the help of new friends and the assistance - including psychological- of the association, the girl tried to leave the pain she will never forget behind her. She began to study, learning the first rudiments of education, starting from scratch. In fact, she was illiterate at the time of her marriage.

Now she wants to give a positive direction to her life. She dreams of engaging in politics to put actions and laws in place that prevent other women suffering as she suffered. She wants to give back the good and the help received. Instead she intends to forget the wickedness so that it's no longer part of her reality and her thoughts.


## Maha, from dolls to a husband

"My father made me get married because he had heard about a rape and he was afraid it might happen to my sister and me as well. I didn't have a choice."
This is what Maha says, a thirteen-year-old who got pregnant at a very young age. Her husband, Abdullah, is ten years older than her. Both are Syrian refugees fleeing the war, who found refuge in Jordan. Abdullah, young Maha's husband, also tries to explain the reasons for child marriages: "If we were still in Syria - he says - we wouldn't have got married, she's too young. But there were often rape attacks in the camp where we live and her father was afraid it might also happen to Maha".

In these places, every day you try and find protection from the bombs, and it's difficult to do so and survive, but no more difficult than trying to defend yourself from poverty and fear of violence.
These are the main reasons why a high number of parents force their daughters into child marriages.
In a quarter of the marriages registered in Jordan amongst the Syrian refugee population the bride is under eighteen, reports *Save the Children* that has

collected data and testimonies by the baby brides in its dossier "Too young to marry".

Child marriages were always fairly widespread in Syria before the war, when approximately 13% of brides were little more than children.
Then when war broke out the phenomenon increased exponentially. Nowadays in Jordan approximately 25% of Syrian brides are younger than 18, and in about half the cases the girls are forced to marry men at least ten years older than them.
The phenomenon is on the increase if you consider that in 2011 the marriages involving a baby-bride were 12% of all marriages. That number increased to 25% in 2013, and this tendency - that includes a quarter of the female population - has remained the same over the following years.


## Maha and Abdullah, spouses against their will

"My future has been stolen from me - says Maha with a hint of sadness in her eyes - and my life is lost. This is not what I dreamt of for myself. I didn't want to shut out every possibility of looking towards the future with the hope of being happy".[1]
What does happiness mean for Maha, if not being able to study, become emancipated and achieve financial independence?
Like her many girls, due to forced and child marriage, have to leave school, and stop dreaming

of living in a better society, in a place where women's rights, and the rights of people in general, are respected.

In the Zaatari refugee camp, in the semi-desert area of the largest camp that exists in the north of Jordan, 80 thousand refugees live in precarious conditions. Some live by the day hoping for government aid to survive and some, to give meaning and organisation to their lives, launch business ventures, small shops offering poor things or small craft enterprises.

In one of the thousands of tents in the camp we find Nadia, another child bride just 15 years old who, like Maha and many others, is aware she does not have a future:

"Ever since I was a child - says the girl - I dreamt of studying nutrition at university. I dreamt of a house and I planned to get married only after completing my education. Instead, my future has been stolen from me and my life is lost. Everything has been destroyed".[2]

It's not always possible to come to the rescue of these young girls who would be so interested in growing, developing themselves and planning their own lives.

For some years now there have been numerous organisations that have implemented programmes to help children in war zones, or otherwise support young people living in rural areas where it is difficult to survive: Amnesty International, Unicef, Save the Children, Amref.

In 2011 the Elders - an international organisation of pacifists and human rights defenders - launched a global partnership against child marriages called *Girls Not Brides*, which currently includes more than a thousand associations that work for the common goal of abolishing child marriage by the year 2030.

This project is highly involving for anyone who feels committed to fighting for the rights of the weakest. The group I belong to has joined *Girls Not Brides* and is strongly motivated. So, the monitoring centre for the safeguarding of equal opportunities (Onerpo) chaired by Aura Nobolo, is among the organisations fighting for this principle of civilisation.

Working in partnership through social networks, we disseminate the group's aims and initiatives on the Facebook page "No more child brides" (*#maipiùsposebambine*).

Based on the network shares we immediately realised that there is considerable sensitivity on the part of men and women who, like us, hope for decisive action at all levels, both national and international, so the common project to abolish child marriage in every country in the world is fully achieved.

# Child marriages in Mexico. The story of Itzel married at 14 years old

Itzel met Jesùs when they were children. She liked him and fell in love with him at 14, when he was a handsome boy of seventeen, as happens to lots of girls, all over the world.  But this was Mexico and adolescents often get married at a very early age. According to United Nations information 6.8 million Mexican citizens are married before age 18.

Itzel married Jesús, convinced by her family that this was the best thing to do for the good of them all. But the girl didn't know her choice would affect her for the rest of her life.
She left school and stayed at home to do the housework and look after the animals.
Her life was spent in loneliness, in a small house, with a little bit of countryside around it.
The days were monotonous and tiring, lived with little enthusiasm and no smiles; lots of duties, very few rights. But nobody could take away her right to dream: to imagine her life could be different, to remember how carefree she was before, when she could go out, go and see her friends, joke with them, go for walks, go to school.
Itzel remembered that at one time she had wanted to be more informed and educated, learn a profession and have a job; but now she was just a goat keeper.
As she ate her frugal meal alone, Itzel was sad and would have liked to tell all young girls: "Think very

carefully before you get married. Above all, remember to study. I regret not having continued my education now and I wonder if life will ever give me another chance. I would so like to go back school".[3]

Not really fully understanding the problem of child marriage, Itzel experienced it first-hand and realised she had precluded any possibility of personal growth for herself. She therefore decided to follow the advice of a former classmate and turned to an association to obtain logistical support to get out of that situation. She was welcomed and helped so she was able to attend some training courses, regain her self-esteem and start to think of a better future.

The *Girls Not Brides* organisation, which is present in Mexico as everywhere else in the world, is very effective at supporting these lost girls who don't know who to turn to. Often in the villages, acquaintances and family members tend to convince the girls that theirs is an unavoidable fate, while in actual fact they are only adolescents or very young girls with their whole life ahead of them.
Without help they certainly couldn't do anything but submit to the wishes of their relatives, and this is why the associations' work is increasing significantly. The measures to assist these girls begin with a preventive action, aimed at preventing them from being forced to leave school to get

married. This action is aimed at families, with meetings in the villages, where all the dangers that arise from child marriage are explained and described. Through documentaries, examples and direct testimonials the parents are made to understand that pregnancies at a very young age entail many dangers. The risks that girls face when they give birth to a child before age 18 are explained to them, ranging from spontaneous abortion, infant mortality, to serious health consequences during and after pregnancy.

The commitment of the activists of the humanitarian associations is constant, and is targeted at very poor families who live in rural areas of Mexico such as Chiapas, Guerrero and Veracruz, where without support they would have absolutely no chance to improve their condition and understand that 40% of the population married at an early age represents a human problem that weighs on the entire social economy.

**Nujood, the courage to divorce at 10 years old**

"I want a divorce." This was the unpredictable declaration of a little girl who stood before the judge and expressed her intention to free herself from the noose of her marriage.
Nujood Ali, born in a small village in Yemen in 1998, is co-author of a book about her story

translated into 17 languages, and is the youngest divorcee in the world.

Because of the family's poverty - when the girl was only nine years old - her father accepted a marriage proposal of a thirty-year-old. So Nujood Ali was forced to leave school to be a wife. She left her family and went to live with her groom.

She cleaned the house, spending her days between daily sexual violence alternated with beatings, which her husband didn't spare her even in the presence of his own mother, who, not only did not defend her, but supported the man's right to do what he wanted to the little girl's detriment.

Nujood Ali was only ten years old and only recently married when she decided she had had enough. She wanted to escape the harassment of a husband in his thirties who had taken away the disenchantment of being a child and made her fall into a kind of hell.

It was a woman in her family who helped her, giving her precious advice. Dowla, her father 's second wife, who told her to run away and go in search of a law court.

So she ran away. Having reached a court she asked a magistrate to help her. A complaint was lodged and in the meantime Nujood Ali was housed in the home of another magistrate who then asked an association that fights child marriage to intervene.

The centre's activists, supported by a lawyer, started legal proceedings that would be an example to many other girls in the same conditions.

Nujood Ali went against her own family, who made her marry to obtain a modest dowry from her betrothed, and at the same time get rid of a mouth to feed at home.

The lawyer *Chadha Nasser*, who defended Nujood Ali free of charge, accused her husband of having broken the law by raping the little girl, and her father of having lied about his daughter's age.

During the debate Nujood Ali refused the judge's proposal to return to her husband after an interval of five years. She couldn't stand that man, or his family, any more.
Nujood Ali got a divorce. It was the 15 April 2008. Her story is told in a book entitled "I am Nujood, age 10 and divorced" written by Nujood and the journalist Delphine Minoui.[4]

The book, distributed with huge success and translated into 17 languages, was made into a film by the director Khadija Al Salami, a victim herself - a former child bride - of an identical fate and a similar escape from a tyrant husband.

Nujood Ali's story is personal and intensely narrated against the background of a rural environment in Yemen, similar to many other developing countries where the rights of girls and women are not recognised; where it seems that nobody pays any attention to the pain a little girl feels when, deprived of her childhood, her dreams, her plans for a happy life, she finds herself a prisoner of a man, in a house, a place, that all darken her very existence.

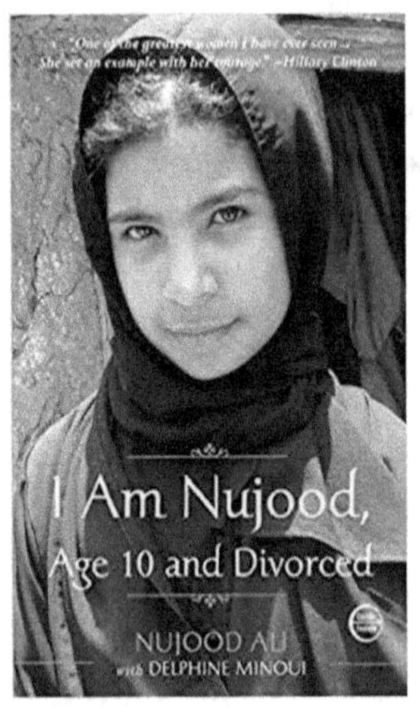


The book and the film on Nujood Ali are at the same time a warning and a journey of hope towards a better, freer, more humane and just society, without abuse and bullying at the expense of the weakest. A society open to total change to achieve the dream of many little girls: a society where everyone has rights. A society freed of poverty and the need to sell its own children.

## Khadija, also a child bride, before she became a successful film director

Khadija Al-Salami, was born in 1966 in Sana'a, the capital of Yemen. At 11 years old she was forced to marry a man of thirty, but did not accept what she experienced as an abuse; and it was, despite her tribe and her family considering marriages between little girls and adults of even thirty or forty years older, legitimate and normal.

The child refused to have sex with her husband and he returned her to her family, as if she were damaged goods.

One day Khadija plucked up all her courage and decided to be the protagonist of her own life, to get divorced and choose to make herself a better person, possibly a happy one.

She ran away from her husband, went to an association for the protection of women, which helped her find work at a local TV station. It was the start of her recovery, her entrance into a work environment that she liked very much and that was to mark the course of her studies, her work and her success as a director.

A providential scholarship, won at 16, helped her achieve her objectives. She went to study in the United States and graduated with top marks in Film Production and Directing.

Then she went to live in France, where she began her career as a documentary filmmaker. She has made dozens of films on the role of Yemeni women and girls.

There have been many rewards in recognition of her commitment in defence of child brides. She was nominated as a *Knight of the Order of Arts and Letters* by Frédérick Mitterrand, Minister of Culture and Communication at that time. She has received accolades from many institutions including the *Foreign Legion*.

Her film "I am Nujood, age 10 and divorced" won an award at the International Film Festival in Dubai in 2014.

Khadija Al-Salami, is the first female Yemeni film director and stands for the commitment and courage of the women of her country. She is an example for all the girls who do not wish to submit to cruel, old fashioned, rural customs which out of ignorance trample their basic rights to live in freedom without being abused.

## Malala Yousafzai, the Nobel Prize girl

Malala is convinced that girls are entitled to an education. She was ten years old when the Swat valley, the District of Pakistan where she lived, was attacked by the Taliban that abolished the right to study with the closure of many schools, including her own.
Malala described life under Taliban rule in a BBC blog using the pseudonym Gul Makai. It was 1999. The girl began several collaborations with major newspapers, including the "New York Times", where she expressed her disagreement with Taliban rule, opposed to education for all Pakistani citizens, especially women.
She on the contrary loudly affirmed during interviews: "I want to go to school, I want to play, listen to music, sing!".

In 2012, she became a Taliban target.

"Which one of you is Malala Yousafzai?" was the question she heard, but didn't have time to answer before two gun shots hit her head. Two armed men had boarded the school bus that was taking her home, with the intention of killing her for having written in her Urdu blog that women have a right to education.

Malala's topics were considered obscene by the terrorists who claimed responsibility for the attack with these phrases: "This is a new chapter of obscenity which we must put an end to... she has become a symbol of western culture in the area, which she has openly touted... she considers Obama her ideal leader. Let this be a lesson to her".[5]

In the telephone claim to responsibility for the attack, Ehsanulla, the Taliban spokesman, threatened a new ambush if Malala survived.
Malala indeed hovered between life and death, but she managed to survive. She was transferred to a hospital in Great Britain and recovered. She then decided to remain in the U.K. with her family, to continue her studies and devote herself to her campaign for girl's education.

She's tough. She was brought up with a good education at home. Her father *Ziauddin*, a poet, and a teacher at the *Khushal Public School*, is of a progressive and emancipated mentality. He has always taught her the value of education ever since she was little and has shown a desire, on several occasions, to see his daughter go into politics one day.

The confidence Malala's father had in his daughter's talent encouraged the girl to engage in social activities which she divulged through blogs and the net. So she began to receive awards and new assignments.
She won the *National Youth Peace Prize*, conferred on her by the Pakistani Prime Minister Yousaf Raza Gilani and was subsequently nominated for *the International Children Peace Prize*.
On 12 July 2013, on the occasion of her 16th birthday, she wore a shawl that had once belonged to Benazir Bhutto, to speak at the Headquarters of the United Nations in New York and made an appeal for the right of every boy and every girl to education.

In November 2013 Malala was awarded the *European Parliament's Sakharov Prize for Freedom of Thought*.
President Martin Schulz defined her as 'a global icon of the fight for girls' education".
Moved, Malala said: "I hope that through our unity and our determination we can achieve our goals and help the 57 million children who expect something from us, who do not want an iPhone, xbox, PlayStation or chocolate, but just want a book and a pen."

Malala's growth programme was set to achieve its highest levels, when beaming, in 2014, she announced on Twitter that she had been admitted to Oxford University: "I'm very excited," she wrote. She was happy to achieve her dream of being able to study. On her website *www.malala.org*, through a non-profit organisation, she collects funds for educational programmes throughout the world.

On 10 October 2014 Malala was awarded the Nobel Peace Prize together with the Indian activist Kailash Satyarthi. She was seventeen years old and the youngest winner of a Nobel Prize *for the struggle against the suppression of children and young people and for the right of all children to education.*


## The story of Aberash. The courage to change

Aberash was 14-years-old, a teenager, when she was kidnapped by a 29-year-old farmer who took her to a hut and brutally raped her.

The man's intention was to force her into marriage. He hoped to get her pregnant and make use of the rule derived from *telefa*, which according to ancient tradition makes kidnapping socially acceptable when the misdeed is followed by a wedding to put things right.

The girl, however, had no intention of yielding to such an imposition, nor to overcoming the affront she had suffered.

She was left alone in the hut and when her kidnapper left, promising to return soon, she realised there was a gun in the house. It belonged to her tormentor who used to hang it on a hook. Aberash, who hated that prison, took the gun and fled.

Her kidnapper returned home and realised that the girl was not there, so he looked for her with some of his friends. He found her and tried to grab her, but she wriggled free, then she fired the gun and killed him.

The story took place in 1996, in Ethiopia, in a rural area, many hours journey away from the capital Addis Ababa.

Aberash was accused of murder. She had the entire village against her, including the kidnapper's mother who found it natural to abduct a girl to then marry her. "It's something everybody does - she said - because it's part of our tradition".

The trial ended two years later with an acquittal for legitimate defence, and the case of Aberash gave rise in Ethiopia, to a provision which considers anyone who kidnaps a woman, for the purpose of forcing her to accept a remedial marriage, as an outlaw; even more so if the case involves a child.

This was a legal breakthrough of utmost importance in a society that has always considered the kidnapping of adolescents and subsequent forced marriage permissible.

The role of the lawyer *Meaza Ashenafi* was decisive for the success of the trial. The legal defence and help of the association of women lawyers (*Andinet Women Lawyers Association*) - founded by *Ashenafi* herself - obtained an effective result that symbolised the redemption of the wrongs suffered by Aberash, and was a warning for those who mistakenly believed they could use violence against girls with impunity.

Once she had released Aberash, Meaza Ashenafi entrusted her to the association she co-founded, for a journey of assistance to overcome the pain still alive in her heart.
 However, the girl had to leave home, her family and go to Addis Ababa to be far away from the accusations of the inhabitants of her village.
It was too risky to remain in a place where her kidnapper's father demanded that Aberash be killed and buried next to his son.
The new criminal code and an acquittal do not serve to make it clear to the tribal society in which the unfortunate fact happened that the inalienable rights of women and girls do exist: self-determination, the right to study, to choose their own destiny. Democratic principles which Aberash's father, the village teacher, and a few others, argued with drawn swords in defence of the girl. Two men as allies in a patriarchal society may be just enough to hope for a better future, and Aberash trusts in the support of those who understand her, to dream of a change in her life

and in the lives of the other girls who live in her country.


## Meaza Ashenafi: the fight for women's rights

Ms. Ashenafi, the lawyer responsible for Aberash's acquittal, has campaigned for many years for legal reform on public education and information for the rights of women and girls.
Born in 1964 in Ethiopia, in a rural village 800 km from Addis Ababa, she was brought up by her father - the mayor of his town - with firm educational principles and a schooling plan for her, her brothers and her sisters.
Meaza soon realised that she wanted to study law. At 17 she was admitted to the University of Addis Ababa, and was the only girl in a class of fifty men, just as in 1986, she was the only woman who graduated in law at her university.
Meaza Ashenafi is currently involved in the work of the *African Centre for Gender at the United Nations Economic Commission for Africa*, and in the creation of the African Women's Rights Observatory.

And in November 2018 her appointment was announced as head of the Supreme Court, the highest legal institution in the country. The Ethiopian Parliament unanimously approved her candidacy.

After the recent historical election of Zewde Sahle-Work to the presidency, the country in the Horn of Africa chose a woman for the first time for such a prestigious role.

Ethiopia is changing, including under the pressure of Prime Minister Abiy Ahmed who gave impetus to his country's reform programme by deciding that 50% of the executive of Addis Ababa should be composed of women.

A fine example for all African countries which can consider the patriarchal model of marginalisation of women in political and institutional roles outdated.

## Difret, the courage to change

Aberash's story inspired the film "Difret, the courage to change", in which the little girl is called Hirut Assefa. The film's narrative is inspired by the true story of Aberash Bekele.

Produced by Angelina Jolie and directed by Zeresenay Berhane Mehari, the film was presented in the United States, where a petition of 135 thousand signatures was delivered to Catherine M. Russell, US Ambassador for global women's issues, by the international organisation *Girls Not Brides*, which interacts in various fields on the problem of child marriages.

In the summer of 2018, from the 25 to 27 June in Malaysia, *Girls Not Brides* convened the largest gathering of civil society supporters committed to putting an end to child marriage.

The organisation's common goal is to allow all girls, all over the world, to realize their potential. To feel free to choose what is best for their life: to study, to gain professional experience, to grow up believing in themselves.

## A film to let the world know about the strenuous fight against child marriages

*Difret, the courage to change* is considered a commendable film. Below is the online review published on "Game Surf ":

"Women's emancipation is a topic that cinema has begun treating in an increasingly disruptive way - writes Roberto Vicario listing various western films on this subject - *Difret, the Courage to Change*, however focuses on what is, perhaps, an even more dramatic topic when compared to the emancipation that western women fight for, and that is the total annihilation of any human right, tied to outdated, ancestral rites that many towns and villages in Africa (but not only!) still use today. To be able to portray the status of women with a clear eye and strong critical sense, the director Zeresenay Berhane Mehari - resident in the US, but born in Ethiopia - leads us, through the eyes of the camera, to live a true story that really happened in his country of origin ".

The choice of the film's title is in itself an exhortation to look with optimism to the future, in fact in Ethiopian the name Difret means courage, and the film is meant to be an encouragement to fight together to change things.


"*Difret - The Courage to Change* - emphasises Roberto Vicario -  is a film that, we are sure, will be uncomfortable for many, especially in its country of origin and in other countries that use similar practices. A film conceived many years ago, which experienced various production problems, almost to its permanent cancellation.
It was Angelina Jolie who, being increasingly active herself in the social field, revived the fortunes of this project and fascinated by the story and the subject decided to take part as co-producer. A happy choice not only for the significance and value of the film - capable even of winning the Sundance Festival - but mainly because from possible cancellation we progressed to a media attention, which can only be beneficial to the production. On the other hand, as the film's title says, we must never stop fighting, but fight with courage to defend our rights, but more than anything else our dreams."[6]

# A petition film

The success of "Difret the courage to change", the film produced in the US with a strong emotional and cultural impact, has not just happened overnight but is the result of many initiatives that preceded and followed the distribution of the work throughout the world. These include the essential initiative of the 1 October 2015, when *Girls Not Brides* launched *#mylifeat15*, an international campaign calling on governments to make it a primary goal to put an end to child marriage by 2030.

## Girls Not Brides, global meeting 2018

*We celebrated reaching 1000 members with a Group photo at our Global Meeting. Photo credit: Graham Crouch/Girls Not Brides*

In Kuala Lumpur, during the second *Girls Not Brides* global meeting, about a thousand organisations from over 70 countries gathered to discuss the issue of child marriage.

The event was overwhelming and participation strongly felt. The interventions, which focussed on achieving the goal of abolishing child marriage by 2030, developed future theories of commitment planning to work collectively at local, national, regional and global levels.

Given the encouraging results already obtained, the effective words of Lakshmi Sundaram, executive director of *Girls Not Brides*, opened up hopes of possible short and long term achievements of goals even more.  Her report, published on the *Girls Not Brides* portal, highlighted the significant commitment on the part of all the partnership's organisations:

"Members - wrote Lakshmi - have been able to effectively share learning, conduct joint advocacy, change local attitudes, influence national and regional strategies, leverage new resources, hold governments accountable and build South-South collaboration. However, for partnerships to thrive and have the greatest impact, they need to include a diversity of voices and be managed effectively".

**Young people are key change-makers.**

"During the global meeting - Lakshmi specified - youth activists shared examples of how their work has led to concrete changes in the lives of girls. It was clear that if we want to end child marriage, we have to empower youth and youth-led organisations and ensure they have the agency to make decisions about their present and future". And it is precisely the commitment of girls who have suffered and experienced child marriage that is one of the drivers of the global project, because, according to Lakshmi Sundaram, they "are amongst the most powerful advocates in efforts to end child marriage, but they need appropriate support to share their stories safely and effectively. They must also be involved in designing policies and programmes to address the issue.

This is why it's critical that the global movement to end child marriage *Girls Not Brides* doesn't just focus on prevention – we have to address the needs of married girls in a holistic manner. To this end we must address gender inequality - stated Lakshmi - it must be at the heart of everything we do, since such discrimination is the fundamental cause of child marriage. And it is important to involve men and boys who can be a key part of the solution to the problem. (...) However, we need to have the courage to discuss some of these difficult topics – including sexuality, social norms and power and race dynamics – openly and respectfully. We're not going to make progress on ending child marriage if we're not willing to take these conversations beyond the Global Meeting". [7]

## Memory Banda: I'll marry when I want

Memory's story is called *"A warrior's cry against child marriage"*.
I'll tell it to you because it's very engaging and also fun to listen to. The video is posted on YouTube (with translations into 38 languages). Just enter the name Memory Banda into the search engine to find it.
I write "fun" because this girl really is a force of nature. She is able to describe with firmness, a sense of humour and courage the enormous problem of a marriage which they wanted to make her accept at all costs.
Her story takes place in Malawi, a country in East Africa. Read what the girl says:

*"When I was 13 years old, I was told: 'You are grown up, you have now reached the age when you're supposed to go to the initiation camp'. I was like: 'What? I'm not going to go to the initiation camp'.*
*You know what the women said to me? 'You are a stupid girl. Stubborn. You do not respect the traditions of our society, of our community'. (...)"*

This teenager's positive energy is exceptional, for not only did she manage to avoid her own marriage, but she fought to have laws passed, to interest public opinion and the institutions of her country. She's organised sit-ins with her friends to get in touch with the relevant authorities to deal with the unfortunate problem of child brides.

Memory tells her story directly to a meeting:

**This is her public speech:**

*"I'll begin today by sharing a poem written by my friend from Malawi, Eileen Piri. Eileen is only 13 years old, but when we were going through the collection of poetry that we wrote, I found her poem so interesting, so motivating. So I'll read it to you. She entitled her poem 'I'll marry when I want'.*

### I'll marry when I want

*'I'll marry when I want.*
*My mother can't force me to marry.*
*My father cannot force me to marry.*
*My uncle, my aunt, my brother or sister,*
*cannot force me to marry.*
*No one in the world can force me to marry.*
*I'll marry when I want.*
*Even if you beat me,*
*even if you chase me away,*

*even if you do anything bad to me,*
*I'll marry when I want.*

*I'll marry when I want,*
*but not before*
*I am well educated,*
*and not before I am all grown up.*
*I'll marry when I want'.*

*This poem might seem odd, written by a 13-year-old girl, but where I and Eileen come from, this poem, which I have just read to you, is a warrior's cry.*
*I am from Malawi. Malawi is one of the poorest countries, very poor, where gender equality is questionable.*
*Growing up in that country, I couldn't make my own choices in life. I couldn't even explore personal opportunities in life.*

**I will tell you a story of two different girls**

*I will tell you a story of two different girls, two beautiful girls. These girls grew up under the same roof. They were eating the same food, sometimes, they would share clothes, and even shoes. But their lives ended up differently, in two different paths.*
*The other girl is my little sister. My little sister was only 11 years old when she got pregnant. It's a*

*hurtful thing. Not only did it hurt her, even me. I was going through a hard time as well.*

*As it is in my culture, once you reach puberty stage, you are supposed to go to initiation camps. In these initiation camps, you are taught how to sexually please a man. There is this special day, which they call "Very Special Day" where a man who is hired by the community comes to the camp and sleeps with the little girls.*

*Imagine the trauma that these young girls go through every day. Most girls end up pregnant. They even contract HIV and AIDS and other sexually transmitted diseases.*

*For my little sister, she ended up being pregnant. Today, she's only 16 years old and she has three children. Her first marriage did not survive, and...*

**On the other side, there is this girl.**

*On the other side, there is this girl. She's amazing.*

*I call her amazing because she is. She's very fabulous. That girl is me. (laughter from the audience)*

*When I was 13 years old, I was told: 'You are grown up, you have now reached the age when you're supposed to go to the initiation camp'. I was like: 'What? I'm not going to go to the initiation camp!'.*

*You know what the women said to me? 'You are a stupid girl. Stubborn. You do not respect the traditions of our society, of our community'.*
*I said no because I knew where I was going. I knew what I wanted in life. I had a lot of dreams as a young girl. I wanted to get well educated, to find a decent job in the future. I was imagining myself as a lawyer, seated on that big chair* (laughter from the audience).


## I knew what I wanted in life

*Those were the imaginations that were going through my mind every day. And I knew that one day, I would contribute something, a little something to my community. But every day after refusing, women would tell me: 'Look at you, you're all grown up. Your little sister has a baby. What about you?'*

*That was the music that I was hearing every day, and that is the music that girls hear every day when they don't do something that the community needs them to do.*
*When I compared the two stories between me and my sister, I said: 'Why can't I do something? Why can't I change something that has happened for a long time in our community?'*

*That was when I called other girls just like my sister, who have children, who have been in class but they have forgotten how to read and write. I said to them: 'Come on, we can remind each other how to read and write again, how to hold the pen, how to read, to hold the book'.*

*It was a great time I had with them. Nor did I just learn a little about them, but they were able to tell me their personal stories, what they were facing every day as young mothers. That was when I was like: 'Why can't we take all these things that are happening to us and present them and tell our mothers, our traditional leaders, that these are the wrong things?'*

*It was a scary thing to do, because these traditional leaders, they are already accustomed to the things that have been there for ages. A hard thing to change, but a good thing to try.*

*So we tried. It was very hard, but we pushed. And I'm here to say that in my community, it was the first community after girls pushed so hard to our traditional leader, and our leader stood up for us and said no girl has to be married before the age of 18!*

*That was the first time that a community had to call the by-laws, the first by-law, that protected girls in our community.*

## We did not stop there. We were in Parliament every day

*We did not stop there. We forged ahead. We were determined to fight for girls not just in my community, but even in other communities. When the child marriage bill was being presented in February, we were there at the Parliament house. Every day, when the members of Parliament were entering, we were telling them: 'Would you please support the bill?' And we don't have much technology like here, but we have our small phones. So we said: 'Why can't we get their numbers and text them?' So we did that. It was a good thing. So... when the bill passed, we texted them back: 'Thank you for supporting the bill!'.*
*And when the bill was signed by the president, making it into law, it was a plus. Now, in Malawi, 18 is the legal marriage age. From 15 to 18!*

## Don't we hear cries of women and girls every day?

*It's a good thing to know that the bill passed, but let me tell you this: There are countries where 18 is the legal marriage age, but don't we hear cries of women and girls every day? Every day, girls' lives are being wasted away.*
*This is high time for leaders to honour their commitment. In honouring this commitment, it means keeping girls' issues at heart every time.*

*We don't have to be subjected as second, but they have to know that women, as we are in this room, we are not just women, we are not just girls, we are extraordinary. We can do more.*

*And another thing for Malawi, and not just Malawi but other countries: The laws which are there, you know how a law is not a law until it is enforced? The law which has just recently passed and the laws that in other countries have been there, they need to be publicized at the local level, at the community level, where girls' issues are very striking.*
*Girls face issues, difficult issues, at the community level every day. So if these young girls know that there are laws that protect them, they will be able to stand up and defend themselves because they will know that there is a law that protects them.*
*And another thing I would say... is that girls' voices and women's voices are beautiful, they are there, but we cannot do this alone.*


## Male advocates, they have to jump in

*Male advocates, they have to jump in, to step in and work together. It's a collective work. What we need is what girls elsewhere need: good education, and above all, not to marry whilst 11.*
*And furthermore, I know that together, we can transform the legal, the cultural and political*

*framework that denies girls of their rights. I am standing here today and declaring that we can end child marriage in a generation. This is the moment where a girl and a girl, and millions of girls worldwide, will be able to say: '**I will marry when I want**'.*

Thank you'.[8]

CHAPTER II


ARE THINGS CHANGING FOR GIRLS?


**People are starting to understand**

Memory Banda's speech ended with a standing ovation, and it is a message of hope for all girls, as well as a keynote speech.
The young men and women at the forefront will be the supporters of the change towards a more just society, and the strategy of the organisations that deal with these issues is based precisely on the impulse the new generations can send to taint the rural social classes with their old fashioned patriarchal mentalities.

The *Girls Not Brides* global initiative with its many hundreds of associations that share the project to abolish child marriage is gradually producing results. Governments in areas at risk seem to be starting to become aware of the serious problem, which is one of social and economic importance. There are many publications which demonstrate the collective costs of non-acculturation of girls, the damage to their health as a result of abortions, premature births, and post-partum consequences.

## *Girls Not Brides* and its partnership international organisations

On the 22 June 2017, the United Nations Human Rights Council recognised the need to tackle child marriage, for the first time, by adopting a resolution proposed by the Netherlands and Sierra Leone, supported by 85 countries, including Italy.
The process to arrive at this UN decision took years of commitment by associations, institutions and governments in every part of the world.

The UN legislation of the 20 November 1989 is the basis of children's rights (*Convention on the Rights of the Child*), and applies to all children, regardless of race, sex, language, religion, opinion of the child/teenager or their parents.
Just as Article 37 of the Istanbul Convention is also important, which with regard to forced marriage states: "The Parties shall adopt the necessary legislative or other type of measures to punish the intentional act of forcing an adult or child to marry".
Approved by the Committee of Ministers of the Council of Europe the Agreement was signed on the 11 May 2011.
Turkey was the first country to ratify it, followed by Albania, Portugal, Montenegro, Moldova, Italy,

Bosnia and Herzegovina, Austria, Serbia, Andorra, Denmark, France, Finland, Spain, Sweden.


## The associations' commitment

In 2016, during the initiatives for the protection of equal opportunities, we lobbied the Italian institutions with Onerpo to raise awareness on the subject of the resolution presented to the General Assembly of the United Nations.
We asked, as affiliates of the *Girls Not Brides* Organisation, to ensure that Italy was seen as a sponsor of the resolution.
Ambassador Sebastiano Cardi, Permanent Representative of Italy to the United Nations in New York, gave us ample reassurance on the uniqueness of the Italian institutional interventions, and on the 23 November 2016 he answered us with a letter detailing how the resolution had been adopted:

*"Italy - wrote Ambassador Cardi - this year was again part of the transregional 'core group' of sponsoring countries. In this capacity we played a proactive role and encouraged dialogue with other delegations to achieve the final result, in particular on some aspects of the new text, such as recognition of the higher risk of child marriage and forced marriage to which children are exposed in humanitarian emergencies, and the need for all Member states to raise the minimum*

*age for marriage within their own jurisdictions,
taking it towards the age of majority. [...]* [9]

The resolution on the unique commitment of
member States, submitted during the Third
General Committee of the United Nations, had a
subsequent passage for its approval by the UN
General Assembly. The 22 June 2017 resolution is
valuable because it recognises child marriage as a
violation of human rights, it calls for a
strengthening of efforts and comprehensive plan to
prevent, punish and eliminate this harmful and
discriminatory practice.

## The passage through Parliament

On several occasions, the Italian Parliament has
developed initiatives to fight the practice of child
and forced marriages.
In parliamentary interventions in the Chamber of
Deputies, documents have referred to various
actions by foreign states, to bring our country's
plan into line with consistency and common goals. [10]

In fact, according to an excerpt from the
parliamentary proceedings "[...] *in 1994, the 179
Governments represented at the Cairo
Conference on population and development had
recognised the direct link between child marriage,
teenage pregnancies and high rates of maternal
mortality, and had emphasised the crucial role of*

*education in prevention actions; in the said Conference's action programme the signatory Governments had committed themselves to protecting and promoting the right of adolescents to receive education on reproductive health and to guarantee universal access to this information; the Convention on the Rights of the Child explicitly recognises children (i.e. persons aged between 0 and 18) as holders of rights and Article 16 of the Convention on the elimination of all forms of discrimination against women (Cedaw) mentions the right to be protected from child marriage; many countries, including those where this practice is widespread, have set the minimum age for marriage, compulsory education and crimes against minors by law, but traditional or religious norms continue to prevail over national legislation; despite the almost universal declaration of commitment to end the practice, it is estimated that marriages of girls under the age of 15 will continue to be celebrated and that in this decade 50 million girls could risk marrying before that age.*

**The various resolutions**:

*On the 22 October 2014, with a resolution passed unanimously in the foreign and community affairs Committee of the Chamber of Deputies, the Government had essentially already committed itself to urgently undertake any useful initiative against the phenomenon of early and forced child marriages in Iraq.*

*On the 18 December 2014, the United Nations General Assembly adopted its first "substantive resolution" on early and forced child marriage; this resolution includes "substantive" recommendations on which the Member States converged, with reference to initiatives to be undertaken by the United Nations and their agencies, Member States, international organisations, representatives of civil society and other relevant players;*

*On the 2 July 2015, the United Nations Human Rights Council adopted a resolution by consensus on child and forced marriage "to strengthen efforts to prevent and eliminate early and forced marriage", the negotiation of which was co-chaired by Italy and Sierra Leone".*

The document also highlights the intention, during the same parliamentary sitting, to abolish FGM:

*"The action to prevent and eliminate early and forced child marriage, requires as much commitment as the effort put into the global campaign for the elimination of female genital mutilation. According to United Nations data published on the occasion of the international day for 'Zero Tolerance of Female Genital Mutilation', the number of girls who are victims of this practice, which puts their lives seriously at risk, has diminished and the unanimous adoption*

*by the general Assembly of the United Nations of the December 2012 resolution, whereby member states are invited to intensify their efforts for the complete elimination of female genital mutilation, has definitely contributed to the achievement of this result; the issue of forced marriage is a further and not secondary aspect of the action to fight gender-based violence and promote women's rights and women' s empowerment; our country has played a great, internationally recognised role, in the campaign against female genital mutilation, which has given Italy a status of international authority that allows it to carry out an equally important role in the prevention and elimination of early and forced child marriage; our country, together with the other states of the G7 group which met in Brussels on the 4 and 5 June 2014, expressed its decision to promote gender equality, to put an end to all forms of discrimination and violence against women and girls, to put end to early and forced child marriage, and to promote full participation and empowerment of all women and girls".*[11]

## Our Government's commitment on *the 21 July 2014*

On the 21 July 2014 the Italian members of parliament drew up and signed a commitment to adopt the resolution against child marriage, approved by the United Nations General Assembly on 18 December 2014, and the one adopted by the United Nations Human Rights Council on the 2 July 2014.[12]

This was followed by the Government's commitment to uphold any initiatives, in all international fora, to prevent and fight actions that violate the human rights of young girls - including in relation to the atrocious practice of genital mutilation - establishing a new type of crime and legislative measures to fight it such as revocation of the residence permit of parents guilty of having forced their minor daughters to marry.[13]

On the 28 July 2015, the motion against early and forced marriage was approved unanimously in the Chamber of Deputies at the first signing of the Socialist Parliamentarian Pia Locatelli, and moreover was signed by almost all the parliamentary groups.

A further motion on the 4 October 2016 in the Senate, completed the proceedings and action plans to protect children's rights and comply with international laws against early and forced marriage.[14]

## The year 2017. Finally, 17 countries approved national strategies to fight child marriage

In 2017, Lebanon, Jordan, Bangladesh, Benin, Cameroon, India, Indonesia, Kenya, Mali, Senegal, Sierra Leone, South Sudan, Zimbabwe approved plans for intervention and national strategies against child marriage.

To comply with the Convention of the United Nations Assembly, many other countries implemented interventions of a regulatory type to prohibit marriage under 18 years of age.
The Latin American countries (Dominican Republic, Honduras, El Salvador and Guatemala) raised the minimum age for marriage to 18, without exception, and regardless of parental or court consent. Germany and Holland implemented the same in Europe.

Malawi, going in the same direction, amended its constitution (drafted in 2015) and banned child marriage, whilst in India, the Supreme Court ruled that sexual intercourse with an under-age wife is - including in the eyes of the law - rape.

**Burkina Faso, the government says "Stop To Child Brides"**

Among the governments that approved plans of action against the practice of child marriage, Burkina Faso launched its "Strategy for the prevention and elimination of child marriage" with the *Ministry of Social Action and National Solidarity (SNPEME - Stratégie Nationale de Prévention et d"Elimination des Mariages d"Enfants 2016-2025)*.

Being persuaded now that such marriages endanger the health, education and possibilities of achieving the potential of children, the institutions finally chose to adopt effective measures that start with the activation of social and family services and the socio-economic protection of the family. They launched programmes and behaviour monitoring focused on support, strengthening of mechanisms and repression, as well as coordination of the stakeholders promoting this strategy.

A dissuasive cultural action is very important, as is psychological and financial support to prevent girls leaving school early and strengthen their social and cultural growth.
To complete the project, many liaison groups work within rural communities: teachers, health workers, security forces, that on finding situations at risk can take over the case.
Funding is guaranteed by technical and financial partners such as *UNICEF, UNFPA, Burkina Plan,*

*Canadian Cooperation, GIZ Prosad* and many other organisations determined to support the government in this fight to protect children's rights.

**Legislators in Honduras approve a new law that makes marriage between children under 18 illegal under any circumstances**

On Tuesday the 11 July 2017 an historic choice was made in Honduras, with the approval of a new law which made marriage under 18 illegal. Marriages between children of this age are not permitted, even with their parents' consent.
Legislators in Honduras voted unanimously.
*Plan International* expressed the organisation's satisfaction through its spokeswoman *Belinda Portillo,* saying that Honduras has 'made history' by endorsing this important piece of legislation in a country where 25% of youngsters are married prematurely, often with marriages between young girls and older men, especially in rural areas where poverty is greater.

**Iran increases the legal age of marriage for women**

In August 2017, the members of the Iranian Parliament also proposed a plan to increase the legal age of marriage for women. *Fatemeh Zolqadr* is one of the promoter members of parliament who, in coordination with the *country's vice-presidency for Women and Family Affairs*, decided to increase the legal age of marriage for women and establish a series of restrictions to prevent it.

The initiative had the support of the Iranian high cleric, Ayatollah *Nasser Makarem Shirazi*, and this boded well that the population would be more convinced to cooperate given the agreement between political and religious institutions.

They began by prohibiting marriage under the age of 13, discouraging families that up to now had agreed, because of poverty and customs, to child marriage for their daughters.

During the debate on the new legislation, the Iranian Parliament placed the emphasis on the damage that is the result of child marriage and involves not only the girls' lives, but has very high social costs, due to the impediment to emancipation, to the right to study and the diseases as a result of early childbirth.

## Child Marriage costs trillions of dollars around the world

"Child Marriage costs trillions of dollars around the world," writes Rachel Clement on *Girls Not brides*. "We have known for decades that early marriage, defined as a formal or informal union where one or both the parties are less than 18 years old, has a huge cost for girls: it interrupts their childhood, truncates their education and often jeopardises their health and economic welfare. But new research by the ICRW -International Centre for Research on Women- and the World Bank -explained the *Girls Not Brides* representative - demonstrates that there are also huge economic costs for society worldwide. The ICRW has discovered that the use of economic models to calculate the cost of so-called 'women's issues' can be extraordinarily effective in attracting the attention of policy makers. This helps stimulate investment in actions against the destruction of human rights which affect women and girls.

After years of work documenting various strategies to put an end to child marriage, the time has come for us to expose the economic purpose of encouraging action. We have developed a global estimate of the costs. Our work to calculate the costs of maternal mortality and gender-based violence has helped create a macroeconomic case for the impact on investment.

We recently looked closely at the costs on a national level in the various countries where child marriage is common, and the results showed large losses wherever the problem is ignored most [...]."[15]

CHAPTER III

THE PETITIONS, THE APPEALS AND THE WEB IN AID OF LITTLE GIRLS

**An Imam marries a little girl of 11, the photo enrages social media, and the web is in revolt**

The criminal photo does not bear looking at according to the web.
A man of forty-one holding hands with a girl of eleven really cannot be suffered. The picture shows them immediately after their wedding ceremony. The indignation is unanimous against Che Abdul Karim, a trader who, not happy with already having two wives has secretly married a third, a Thai child bride, removing her from school, from her games; tearing her away from her teenage dreams, her right to an education and to live a peaceful childhood.

One of Abdul's wives files a complaint with the Malaysian authorities who open an investigation because, although polygamy is permitted in Malaysia, a person must be at least 17 to get married.

Therefore, in the words of the Deputy-Minister *Wan Azizah Wan Ismail,* the authorities declare the marriage illegal, which among other things had not been approved by the Sharia Court. Abdul on the other hand, who is also the imam of a rural village in the state of *Kelantan*, insists that the marriage is legal, that the child's parents approved it.

The man has six children of varying ages, the eldest is eighteen, much older than the little girl his father has married; if he had even a sliver of conscience he should take not one but a hundred steps back and leave the little girl in peace.


## The child slave

Can a child-slave rebel?  Thank goodness yes. Takira did so, her story full of unhappiness began when her father promised her in marriage to a man double her age.

Takira was 12, she lived in Albania, and once married she became her husband's property. She had two children with him, and looked after them with love. They were her only source of joy in a life full of humiliation and bullying. Then a hope of change illuminated her heart when her entire family, moved to Italy. She thought that far from Albania, a country with lots of child brides without rights, there would be a turning point in her bitter life.

**Journey to Italy**

She did not really know what Italy was, but she had heard of it as a country where prosperity, democracy, respect for human rights are the basis of coexistence.
She hoped there would be an end to her mistreatment, her segregation, the abusive actions of her husband.

She dreamt of being able to go back to school, of having a decent home. She went to live near Rome thanks to a family reunion visa. But she was an illegal immigrant because her husband had registered their children on his residence permit, not Takira. And that is how her husband treated her, as an illegal immigrant, relying on the fact that she could not ask anyone for help, he beat her, he took the little money she earned with an off-the-books job, he threatened to kill her.

The fear of being beaten and killed, and even more of losing her children, paralysed Takira.
Beatings were the order of the day for the most trivial reasons, the children crying, the quality of the wine served at table, the soup which lacked salt. To the man she was a baby factory, an object that belonged to him.

It's difficult to get out of such a situation for someone with very few cultural and information tools available to them. Thanks to the commitment of lots of associations that support girls, who are little more than defenceless children, in some cases we are able to win against the indecent practice of child marriage.

*Differenza Donna* is one of these associations which takes care of them with the help of psychotherapists, social workers and sociologists. Each working in their own role to build a project for a dignified life for every girl in need of help.

Ilaria Boiano, a lawyer - interviewed on this topic - explained that a right only has a function if the victim knows she has it, while most of the time, foreign women do not have this awareness.

In truth, victims are afraid that once a complaint for mistreatment has been lodged they may lose their residence permit, or even that the administrative process concerning them might be cancelled.

The residence permit is aimed, in these cases, at family reunion, but very often husbands do not request, or ever collect, their wife's documents in order to keep her under check: isolated from the social environment, frightened, submissive.

However, since 2013, in order to offer assistance to foreign women, the Italian institutions have established a residence permit provided specifically to victims of domestic violence.

## A friend's help

Takira found out that her rights were protected by law in Italy after she asked a friend, more expert than herself, for information, and having a good knowledge of Italian she accompanied her to lodge a complaint; she reassured her and told her not to fear any kind of deportation because once it has been ascertained that a foreign woman is undergoing violence the Italian authorities help her.

In fact, Italian law provides that - to remove a victim from abuse - the chief of police shall issue a residence permit (Law 119/13 Article 4).

The welcome the girl received from the police officers and the social workers comforted her, and once she had taken a first step into the headquarters of the *Differenza Donna* Association, Takira realised that her troubles were coming to an end.

The assistants skilfully included her in a programme that provided literacy training, information on women's rights, logistical help to get out of her husband's house, and to deal with lawsuits.

So Takira began to breathe again, she resumed her life, learnt Italian, she began working; she felt free from blackmail, fears and violence.

With her children she started a new life where the hope of a better future made the little family serene and grateful to all those who assisted them in order to be able to get away from the oppression of an overbearing husband.

**Hameya, the child bride tortured to death**

How do you tell the story of Hameya?
It is hard to believe that what the small girl suffered could really have happened.
The marriage - if it can be called that - lasted six months, and was described with all its ups and downs by a reliable source like the "Daily Mail".

The story happened in Afghanistan in the province of Baghdis, where a little 7 year-old girl was sold as a "bride" to Asharaf a man of about 30, moreover who already had a wife.
The tribal rite that initiated this devastation of human rights is called 'badal', and it consists in an exchange of children between two families that with a single ceremony save on the costs for the sale of the body of two innocents.
Under the pact, two brothers-in-law exchanged the little girls: Hameya's brother married the sister of Asharaf, and vice-versa the latter married Hameya.

Aside from any moral judgment, the two marriages did not prove to be successful. Discussions and quarrels broke out between Hameya's brother and his wife; disagreements that were exacerbated more every day, until they reached the worst possible outcome: the bride's death.

Hameya's brother killed Asharaf's sister, who had been delivered to him as his wife with the 'badal' rite.

A period of hatred begins between the families, primarily at the expense of Hameya. Only a few months had passed since the so-called wedding ceremony, when Asharaf's revenge began by cruelly maltreating, up to the point of torturing her, his child-bride.

Hameya sought help from her family, but as so often happens in these cases, families send the 'defector' back for two main reasons: a sense of shame towards the village and the bridegroom's family that comes from not maintaining a 'sale agreement', and a refusal to burden themselves again with another mouth to feed.
It should be remembered that for these rural families giving away a daughter in marriage is a liberation from the burden of keeping her, and once a girl has been handed over as a bride her relatives consider it right that her husband should feed her.

However not even Hameya's parents imagined that Asharaf could carry out his revenge to the bitter end.
Hameya met with a horrible end. Asharaf killed her and ran away looking for protection in an area controlled by the Taliban. After the discovery of

Hameya's poor body, the police reached the murderer and arrested him.

An ending and a predictable punishment for an occurrence of unprecedented violence, which it is very difficult to understand how it could have happened. A man approaching a little girl to abuse her should be prevented not only by law, but with a system of social attention to what happens in families at risk; punishments and serious consequences should be provided for anyone who becomes an accomplice and does not intervene to protect innocent children: the family, the neighbourhood, schools, governmental institutions.

The serious crime committed by Asharaf is abhorred by the healthy and conscious part of the country, and by many young people who represent the hope of an evolution in the field of human rights, so that a safety net for children prevents other little girls from suffering what Hameya suffered.

**The story of Rulima in India**

(*Facebook and WhatsApp: campaign against child marriage by a local group of young people*)

Rulima Khatun, lives in Dalgaon in the Darrang district of Assam, a poor, culturally backward neighbourhood. At 17 she ran away from home when her parents insisted she got married to an older man. She took refuge with a friend because she had no intention of giving in and accepting the dictates of her family.

From her hiding place she told her story to a group of local young people who, through word of mouth, found a way to prevent forced marriage.

The young people decided to use modern dissemination tools and began a persuasive campaign to help Rulima. They posted updates on Facebook and WhatsApp. They sent a warning message to a WhatsApp group called *Balya Bibah Birodhi Mancha* (Forum against child marriage). Widespread interest followed with messages published online, all in aid of Rulima.

They garnered the interest of some local politicians and the activists of the *All Assam Minority Student Union* (AAMSU), a student body that stands up for minors.
The marriage was averted. Rulima breathed a sigh of relief, because she finally felt her future could change. She was happy to be a little more in charge of her own life.
The girl's father, Nuru Sheikh, surprised by the clamour his daughter's story had caused, began to meditate on the issue, to ask questions, look for information. His awareness of the issue increased which led him to publicly declare: "It was a

mistake. I see that now and I will never make a mistake like that again."

The move towards the knowledge that children's rights cannot be restricted is rather slow in these places, and not just for girls.

A similar situation happened in Baragua, in the district of Barpeta, where a teenage boy was pushed to marry someone he did not even know because his family had reached an agreement with the relatives of the hypothetical future bride. But in this case too, the marriage fell through thanks to the *network,* and with
the support of the *Balya Bibah Birodhi Mancha* groups, the opinions of the internet communities on Facebook and WhatsApp multiplied, and the clearly contrary and critical comments and phrases made the boy's relatives ashamed of wanting to convince him to marry at all costs.

Ayub Ali, the boy's father, interviewed by local reporters, admitted that he wanted to marry off his youngest son and explained that initially, given their traditions, he saw nothing wrong; then he realised that the world was changing. The protests and comments on social media made him understand he was about to make a big mistake.

**Social media to the rescue (not just bullies from the web)**

At a time when abuse, fraud and scams are rife on social networks, it is comforting to know that a group of girls and boys in Assam are reversing the trend and using the Internet to fight social evils such as forced marriage of minors, so much that they are now feared by those who advocate and practice child marriage.

Ainuddin Ahmed, secretary general of AAMSU (*All Assam Minority Students Union*) is happy to be able to win a huge challenge started in a rural village by young people who use Facebook and WhatsApp.

Articles and interviews covering the stories of Rulima and other group initiatives are published on the *VillageSquare.in* portal:
"I started the AAMSU platform initiative - says a satisfied Ahmed - as an individual who experiences the pathetic condition of society in the uneducated and poor areas. The young people of the student body have supported me in a really big and overwhelming way".

In addition to the AAMSU members, other parties such as various NGOs and police officers, have enrolled in these social media groups, and the possibility of interacting to modernise the country increases every day. However, Ahmed is calling for greater support from government agencies in order to achieve even more incisive and far reaching results.

## A bumpy road full of dangers

The initiatives of the AAMSU group and other Indian organisations working to tackle child marriage, do not have to fight only the ignorance and insecurity of many families, who consider a daughter's marriage as a release from a financial commitment: one less mouth to feed and an easing of the burden of controlling a daughter who could be 'compromised' before marriage.
One major obstacle to the children's rights project is constituted by the wrath of local warriors who sponsor child marriage and go as far as attacking and beating up anyone who does not comply with their wishes.

In an interview with *Village Square* a young man, Ashraful Hussain, explained that when he tried to stop a child marriage near the Barpeta district, the bridegroom's family attacked him together with his friend. They were beaten and kept segregated in a house for days, until one night the police, warned by other friends of the AAMSU group, freed them.

The dangers do not deter these young people, now numerous, who are active through Facebook and WhatsApp. They monitor every event or act of force towards child marriage and, in case of problems, immediately take steps in coordination to deal with them.

AAMSU also organizes awareness campaigns in various locations throughout the country transmitting them live on Facebook. In this way the results can be considered satisfactory because in 2017, over a few months, 250 child marriages were stopped.


**The main reason is poverty**

In Assam early marriages are prevalent among the Muslim and tribal population. In addition to this there is an organisation that distributes money to parents to encourage them to marry off their daughters.

This makes the intention of abolishing practices which harm children's rights more complicated and arduous.

According to the *National Family Heath Survey* (NFHS) in 2015-2016, at least 32.6 per cent of married women aged between 20 and 24 were married before their 18th birthday, and 23.3 per cent of boys, now aged between 25 and 29, were married before they were 21 years old. In addition, at least 14 per cent of girls aged between 15 and 19 years old had become pregnant.

In 1978 Indian law had already established that to marry, girls must be at least 18 years old, while for boys the legal age is 21 years old.

**In Turkey, there is still a lot to be done**

For a long time, Turkey was considered a nation tending towards progress and respectful of egalitarian rights, but recently a male chauvinist culture seems to dominate in the government's actions that considers the practice of child marriage a normal path not to be condemned.
The Turkish Statistics Institute (TurkStat) informs us that in 2016, 17.9% of marriages involved under 18s. Again, in this case too, the conditions of poverty of families living in rural areas affected the results. Moreover, the influx of young refugees from Syria - married very young - and the problems of underdevelopment in the east and south-east of Anatolia, bring to light a large number of stories of suffering and dramatic events like the death of various child-mothers during childbirth or as a result of consequences related to sexual abuse.

In November 2016, the Turkish Government - worsening the situation - drafted a bill that granted men, sentenced for abuse of a minor, absolution through a shotgun wedding.
Immediately right across Europe, as well as in Turkey itself, lots of protest actions began, collections of signatures and petitions to the government to ask it to back down from its proposal. Public opinion - both secular and Islamic in observance - including the women's organisation within the AKP, the Islamic party which governs

Turkey - founded by Erdoğan himself - took to the streets like an irrepressible wave.

Of the Islamic spokespersons, journalist Ayse Bohurler reacted with heavy public statements on Twitter and posted the phrase: "the proposal put forward is neither legal nor does it adhere to the principles of Islam. In Islam sexual abuse is a sin, a crime [...]".

The protest was general with the participation of the Social Democrats of the CHP, the pro-Kurdish HDP, women and men of various social classes; everyone opposed the legalisation of child abuse.

Even Sumeyye Erdoğan Bayraktar, daughter of President Erdoğan - Vice President of KADEM, the women and democracy Association - left punchy declarations contrary to DDL.

Finally, thanks to the impressive number of reactions by such a large part of the public opinion the government had to back off from its decision. The save-rapists bill was withdrawn.

The rules, however, had been there since 2001, the start date of the ban on child marriage. But, even if it is illegal, child marriage still remains prevalent in Turkey.

Over the years, strong action by the NGOs against baby brides has been registered, especially after the death of young Kader, a child married off at just 11 years old, and found dead after the birth of her second child, when she was 14.

This was yet another occasion that caused a wave of outrage in the country.

Research by the NGO Kamer on a sample of 60 thousand women in 23 provinces including Siirt - where young Kader lived - reveals the fact that the percentage of marriages involving minors is 33%. With numerous marriages of girls under the age of 12 in rural villages, where girls are often used as bargaining chips. And we are talking about Turkey, a country that is a candidate for entry into the European Union that should aspire to a different and more modern concept of human rights.

Civil society initiatives manage to obtain small results with great effort and commitment. It will take many more years unfortunately to win against poverty and all the contributing factors that determine such a high percentage of child marriage. There is still a lot to do in Turkey, and much will depend on who governs it.

## Child brides, stories of illegal ceremonies that lead to death

Every year millions of little girls are forced to marry and consequently despite being so small become pregnant, give birth and die. There is no respect for their childhood on the part of those who, by putting their hands on these innocent creatures, perform outright illegal acts of paedophilia.

In developing countries 70 million girls begin married life before reaching the age of majority.

We know that the two contributing factors that determine such behaviour are poverty and ignorance of families who sell their daughters to obtain compensation in cash or in durable goods. They justify their actions by saying that in this way they are protecting the girl's virginity, who with the passage of time could be violated by an ill-intentioned prowler, and guaranteeing her a future in which someone will provide for her livelihood.

So the poor creatures, not to be violated by a contemporary, perhaps during some chance encounter during adolescence, are abused in childhood by adults who are twice or three times their age (when it is not a decrepit and depraved old man), who pay, and feel they have the right to life and death over their 'goods'.

**Let's dispel any romanticism**

Let's remove all sentimentalism, because there are no feelings involved in this appropriation of the childhood and future of these little girls. The child is taken as a sexual object, in a doubly advantageous contract, because in exchange for lunch and dinner, the little girl will also become a housemaid, she will do the cleaning, prepare meals, do the washing, including the sheets on which she will have lain with her tormentor and if her "spouse" has animals, she will also have to look after them. She will be a submissive and obedient "wife" (but I would say slave), and she will keep quiet even when she gets clouted for not having done the housework properly, or simply because the man who has enslaved her is ready with his fists.

Think about how these little girls live: no dolls, no dreams, nor future. Nor is there any fun, excursions, teenage love stories, games with their contemporaries. Books? No way. School? No
Only useful for looking after the goats and lying with the old man.
The damage? A lot, too much, to the psychological and emotional, social and cultural spheres. What can be said? It's like taking a shoot that could flourish and become anything: a teacher, an artist, a doctor, a politician; or a simple shop assistant who loves her job, advises her customers, meets people, has friends and on Sundays goes dancing or to the cinema with them. Instead this little bud is locked in a box, a house where a master rules and where she can only do two things, be a kitchen maid and a sexual object.
And if any children come along, she will be able to experience the joys of motherhood, with a real baby instead of a doll, and also the dangers of an early pregnancy, in which mortality rates for the mother and the unborn child are extremely high. Newborn babies of a child bride have a 60 percent probability

of dying compared to the babies of a woman who is at least twenty years old.

Every year there are 7.3 million child brides who give birth to a baby, running risks because a child's body is not ready for such an effort.
This is a brutal violation of human rights against which more must be done, with strict regulations, preventive actions, awareness in the field of education and culture, in rural communities, in families;
so that being able to go to school and study is no longer a luxury or a practice reserved for the few.

According to statistics released by Unesco, 65 million little girls do not have access to any type of education. So, many of them are offered as brides to men who could be their father, not to say their grandfather. Men who then dispose of the girls as privately owned objects.


**Tanzania, married girls come back to school!**

In sub-Saharan Africa, there is a dual pathway that leads to child marriage. A certain percentage are marriages forced by families, but a survey has shown that it is the girls themselves who, for fear of not being able to keep themselves, decide to get married.
As always, poverty rules supreme and affects the existence of the underprivileged, however even the

ones who choose to marry as adolescents, soon regret having abandoned their studies to find themselves without a future, far from the school environment, their friends, their books.

*Girls Not Brides* has a delegation in the area and has supported the Ministry of Health in conducting a survey with the participation of other organisations like *Plan International, Children's Dignity Forum, FORWARD*.
According to this research, 37% of girls in Tanzania are married before their eighteenth birthday, with high percentages of up to 59% and 58%, (Shinyanga and Tabora) while they go down from 19% and 8% in *Dar es Salaam and Iringa.*

Following the publication of these surveys the Tanzanian government decided to take action to change the situation, by putting in place a range of initiatives, including the enactment of new laws, investments in education, school transport and dissemination of information on the gravity of the problem in order to help rural populations understand the damages caused by early marriage, instead of considering it a solution to overcome their difficulties.

## A step forward and the praise of the UN

In Tanzania it began with popular petitions, to continue with pressure from the associations together with educational and cultural institutions moving towards an awareness raising plan by local government. Until a resolution was obtained against female genital mutilation (FGM) and child marriage.
The Tanzanian government institutions earned the praise of the United Nations, expressed by the spokeswoman Hoyce Temu, in February 2016, in Dar es Salam.
This outcome was also the result of numerous petitions organised around the country on several occasions, including the International Day of Zero Tolerance for FGM, on the 6 February 2016.

These initiatives are absolutely necessary in a country where on average 15 per cent of women have experienced FGM, while in the Manyara region that percentage rises to as much as 77 per cent.
Among other things, Tanzania is a signatory to the International Convention of Peking that committed all adhering governments to respect the prerogatives of young girls, abolish gender discrimination, protect the health of minors and set the global minimum age for marriage at 18.

The United Nations, appreciating the recent trend to protect children, will support the government of

Tanzania in order to eliminate all forms of discrimination and violence against women and girls. In turn, their leaders have joined the sustainable development programme, to deal with key challenges during the twenty-first century, such as poverty, inequality and violence against women.


**The Action Plan in Tanzania**

The national action plan aims to achieve an end to violence against women and children, the dissemination among the population of sexual information, knowledge of their rights, the possibility of refusing to marry, the right to decide the course of their own life.
The encouragement to change things goes as far as persuading married girls to return to school.

The Ministry of Education, civil society organisations, United Nations agencies, community leaders and other stakeholders are all making a case to support the common cause against child marriage.
The uniting of so many people working together with organisation and efficiency has begun to yield tangible results that presumably will improve, betwveen now and the future, if we continue to put in place resources, intelligence and multiple actions planned to achieve the total abolition of child marriage.

## Cartoons to tackle the issue and make it comprehensible to all

An effective approach to the difficult subject of child marriage was invented by "Team Muhafiz" in Pakistan: cartoons to explain the issues and stories of child brides to everyone and especially to young people.

Consequently, a growing number of civil society organisations have chosen to use them and experienced an immediate return in terms of dissemination and participation by families, schools and young girls.

The booklets are easy to read, with colour pictures, and the writing with direct dialogues represents an ideal choice among educational messages.

## New developments in Pakistan with the gimmick of 'advertising' lorries for the right to study

It has to be admitted that Malala Yousafzai's homeland always engages with new ideas to advance the project to abolish child marriage.

The latest in order of time is the invention of advertising carried around by lorry drivers in the most remote corners of the country.

Goods transporting vehicles are commonly panelled with pictures to advertise new films at the cinema, political elections or commercial promotions, but the idea of representing smiling girls with books under their arms and writing the phrase *"Education is a girl's fundamental right. Send your daughters to school"* came to Haji Khan, an intelligent lorry driver, advised in turn by his friend, a painter.

The two discussed the exciting idea, then they got down to work. The painter frescoed a panel which shows a girl dressed in blue, with an open book, the face of a little girl with a fresh smile and expressive eyes that convey joy. The picture's positiveness is of course due to the happiness that the girl expresses at being able to attend school.

Haji Khan's lorry began driving around the cities and villages of Pakistan, reaping enormous success. The idea, picked up by the anthropologist Samar Minallah, was boosted with the help of Unesco and the Asian Bank *ADB*.

But let's see what 'newsd.in' writes:


## "Pakistan: Drivers paint 'studying girl' image on trucks to advocate women's right to education

*In Pakistan, trucks are often used as moving billboards, sporting random images of heroes with guns or females with skimpy clothes, and of course, the all-time quote against the evil eye – 'Buri nazar waale tera muh kaala.' (He who casts the evil eye can be publicly dishonourable). However, in recent times they have come up with a unique idea of using trucks to spread messages about women's rights.*

*Girl's rights are gaining new ground in Pakistan as rights activist and documentary filmmaker Samar Minallah is rallying truck drivers to help spread awareness - through this traditional art - about girls' education across the country, including in the more remote areas.*
*The trucks are now seen carrying huge paintings showing pictures of smiling girls carrying their books.*
*The intention is to give the new generations the right to education, condemning the bad practices of early child marriage.*

*The campaign began when a truck driver, Haji Khan, decided to change the painting on his vehicle from that of a film star to the portrait of a girl carrying a school bag with a smile on her face. The painting also carries an inscription that says 'Education is the basic right of a girl.*
*Send your daughters to school'.*

*According to the magazine 'Gulf News', a truck painter at a workshop in Peshawar suggested to Haji Khan, that he should carry the evocative picture on his truck as it would help curb the negative practice of child marriage;*
*Khan immediately agreed.*

*Truck art is a big source of publicity in Pakistan, and as Khan's vehicle travels from Khyber to Karachi it carries out a sort of targeted advertising, because its target is the rural population where most of the bad practices of child marriage prevail.*
*Samar Minallah, is a social worker, anthropologist, and supporter of this programme. She came up with this idea through discussions with the Asian Development Bank (ADB) and UNESCO, who appreciated the project and are now financing it to increase its 'on the road' dissemination by trucks carrying the 'progress adverts'."* [16]

## Afghanistan, Child brides at 9 years old

While in Pakistan they are trying to fight the scourge of child marriage by resorting to the creation-disclosure of cartoons, or with ingenious inventions such as advertising on trucks, in Afghanistan the road to eradicating it is still a long one.
Tribal traditions, the leadership of many religious, ignorance and enormous poverty induce families to decide to sell their daughters for considerable sums of money.

Research uncovers the seriousness of the situation, according to the Iwpr (*Institute of War and Peace Reporting*), in the provinces of Balkh, Faryab and Jawzan most girls get married between the ages of 9 and 14 years old; this happens even though the minimum age for marriage in Afghanistan is 16, according to law.

Despite attempts to restore lawfulness, local authorities admit to not being able to prevent the phenomenon, let alone the likely consequences such as pregnancy and the serious risks of death during childbirth.

The World Health Organisation, has raised an alert on the phenomenon that records the number of 460 women out of every hundred thousand deaths of minors, every year in Afghanistan, due to complications during childbirth.

**The strategies of Girls Not Brides**

Unfortunately child marriage is practised in many countries around the world by people of different ethnicities and religions. These customs have undermined the potential development of girls in every part of the globe; however, five years ago, the attention of some social parties towards the significant problem led to a programme of interventions for change. The *Girls Not Brides* organisation, with its global partnerships of about a thousand associations, including in Italy the *Onerpo Observatory*, and *Terre des Hommes*, has planned cultural and institutional resolutions to improve the lives of many children and girls.

**Girls Not Brides, the international organisation against child marriage. The associations that support it**

*Photo credit: Girl Up Initiative Uganda.*

*Girls Not Brides*, is a partnership of over 1000 civil society organisations present in Africa, Asia, the Middle East, Europe and the Americas, engaged in putting an end to child marriage with a broad-spectrum action plan aimed at dissemination of the project on a global level, to individually reach every rural area where the problem of child brides exists, such as Egypt, Ethiopia, Nepal, Bangladesh, Burkina Faso, Chad, Ghana, Mozambique, Nepal, Uganda, Zambia and Zimbabwe.

Initiatives against child marriage are progressing at a satisfactory pace where there is availability and willingness to change things on the part of the governments involved, which commit funds and draft bills against the practice of child brides.
Various ministries of the participating countries are involved in the programme: from the ministry of health concerned with reproductive age and the prevention of diseases in the girls, to that of Education to monitor participation in school cycles.
The associations, schools, civil society are of paramount importance, together with the institutions, to assist government actions.

Progress as a result of the initiatives of *Girls Not Brides* is tangible. It can be measured, especially in the last 5 years, in terms of the reduction in cases of child marriage, preparation and approval of legal arrangements and funding, greater attention of politicians and institutions in the places where action is necessary; birth of associations and movements, and greater participation of young people, both boys and girls. As if to demonstrate that the new generations are different or intend to be so compared to the past.


## THE INITIATIVES OF THE VARIOUS GOVERNMENTS


### A Resolution Against Child Marriage by the Belgian Parliament

The Belgian government's resolution in March 2015, tackled the issue of child marriage in countries with marriage rates above 30%.
Consequently, it renewed its cooperation agreement with Niger, the country with the highest percentage of child marriage, and cooperated with Mali, Mozambique, Uganda, Democratic Republic of Congo, Tanzania and Benin.

Immediately after the vote in Parliament, the Deputy Prime Minister and Belgian Minister for Development Cooperation, Alexander De Croo, considered the problem complex: it concerns parents the social context, the poor living conditions.
The Belgian government's resolution supported by *Girls Not Brides*, and *Plan Belgium* rewarded the campaign to put an end to child marriage already launched some time ago.

These and other initiatives are essential for the cause of these little girls. The more forces involved in the field, the greater the possibility of closing the painful chapter of the rights denied to children.

According to figures released by the Organisation *Plan*, if nothing stops this process by 2020 there will be 140 million child brides.

Every day, 39 thousand little girls get married in developing countries, and in no less than 146 countries around the world girls under 18 can marry with the consent of their parents, whilst in 105 countries the phenomenon also involves male children.

These percentages highlight that, in this case as well, discrimination against females does exist, in the total absence of respect for children in general.


**Nepal Girls summit**

(the strange marriage with a tree)

Nepal, in South Asia, has a destiny of its own enclosed in its landlocked territory.

The country shares some customs and a lack of rights with China to the North and India to the South.

Kathmandu is the multi-ethnic capital with a predominantly Hindu and Buddhist population where there is a strange custom on the part of the tribal Newars, the *Ehee* rite for fertility repeated every year, during which little girls between the ages of 5 and 12 are married to a *bael* tree. This is a gift from her father who earns rewards in heaven for having granted his daughter this way before she becomes a woman.

Criticism of this superstitious practice comes from that more advanced and civil society that considers this sort of pre-announcement of a "real" marriage negative for unions between adults and underage children.


**Nepal's government tackles the problem**

On the 23 March 2016, Nepal's government tackled the urgent issues concerning child marriage and female genital mutilation.

After the first summit held in London in July 2014, which was attended by the President of the Republic of Nepal Bidhya Devi Bhandarie and Prince Harry of the United Kingdom, the Nepalese institutions began to worry about these serious problems.

In Nepal, 41 per cent of girls marry before the age of 18 and 10 per cent are already married around the age of 15, most of the time due to poverty, and ancestral customs.

The government of Nepal is aware that it will be difficult to dismantle beliefs and customs if no action is taken against poverty and with a series of initiatives envisaged by a detailed and effective national plan.

**India, declares it is a crime to have sex with an underage wife**

Albeit slowly, one after the other governments where the most underage marriages are celebrated are becoming aware of the serious problem and through laws and sentences are taking the necessary action to put a stop to these cruel ancestral practices.

In India the Supreme Court has ruled that a sexual relationship between a man and his underage wife of between 15 and 18 is considered rape, therefore a criminal offence. The judges took the view that sexual intercourse with persons under the age of 18 are contrary to the law and violate the physical integrity of young girls.
The ruling is the consequence of a complaint by a minor who, assisted by a lawyer, told the Court she had been compelled by force to have sexual intercourse with her husband, an adult and considerably older than her.

CHAPTER IV

## OTHER CASES OF ABUSED GIRLS

## Iraq, Child Brides in Baghdad

**"Iraq, child brides at 9 years old",** *by Giuliana Sgrena*

*"It's happening in democratic Baghdad: A crime against humanity, is how Hanaa Edwar defines it, because it deprives girls of their right to live a normal childhood".*

So begins the article by Giuliana Sgrena of 15 March 2014 on "Globalist", referring to the bill approved by the Iraqi government in February 2013, to lower the legal age of marriage for girls to 9 years old.
The bill proposed by the Minister of Justice, Hassan al Shimari, recalled the Quran code and stated that girls reach puberty at 9 years old, when they can marry.

Abundant protests followed by politicians and civil society at international level, including those of Nickolay Mladenov, the United Nations representative in Iraq, because the law cancelled women's rights guaranteed by international agreements.

Feminist movements and a chorus of national and foreign dissent managed to stop the aberrant paedophile law, called 'Jaafari', that aimed to authorise the lowering of the age for marriage and cancel the 1959 rule of law, which when it was approved during Abdel Karim Kassem's government, after the 14 July 1958 revolution, was considered to be one of the most advanced laws in the world on women's and children's rights.

Unfortunately, in November 2017 before the new parliamentary elections in May 2018, the conservative Shiite Al-Fadhila party re-proposed the rule derived from the Quran.
Subsequently, the Iraqi Parliament let the bill lapse which would have transferred legal competence on the matter from the State to the religious authorities. Fortunately, protests in the country and abroad prevailed, and let us hope that proposals to go backwards in the protection of rights are forever cancelled, as they are deleterious, far from a profound religious sense and far from human values. A country like Iraq, which has a very old culture and tradition, deserves to maintain the secularity of its state, while respecting multiple religious denominations.

## Being a slave, without knowing it

Let's call her Leda, although that is not her real name, which must rightly be protected as in any news story involving children. The story is one of those which, a few years ago, we didn't even imagine could happen in Italy, after years of fighting for equal opportunities, social justice and constitutional principles that very clearly safeguard the rights of minors.

It was 2004, and Leda was 14 years old when her parents sold her to a Kosovar family, much in the same way, no more no less, as if they were selling an object, or a barnyard animal, instead of a young girl.

The events took place in Puglia and Pieve di Cento, a town in the province of the highly intellectual Bologna.

An agreement was quickly reached between Kosovars. The aspiring groom's family made an offer:

 "Would you sell us your daughter? We need to buy a wife for our son."

"How much are you offering?"

"Sixty thousand euros."

"Deal done. Take her".


Now that's a considerable amount of money, and it could well seem that the family wanting to buy the girl was not scrimping in order to marry off their son. However, if we consider that it's an illegal transaction, an abuse of a minor, the price also

covers the risk of acting outside the law, beyond every social convention and in contempt of common morality, not just Italian morality, but the morality of every civil forum.
Observing the story through an impudent eye, Leda's purchase is almost like a commercial investment, because the girl will not just be a teenage bride forced to accept an older man than herself, but - according to her acquired family's plan - she will have to "make" money by begging. Every day she's expected to go on the streets to beg, and not dare return home until she's collected an acceptable amount of takings.

Unable to refuse, Leda began her unhappy married life. At the slightest refusal to obey her "masters", she was beaten black and blue. Her father-in-law, the financial backer of the operation, thrashed her, her husband mistreated her. If Leda, tried to seek solace from her own parents, she was beaten by her father and master. Who was very worried about having to repay the 60,000 euros that the Kosovar in-laws would demand in the event of a breach of the sale.
Leda was trapped: "To walk away from this house" - her husband often told her - "you must pay back the 60 thousand euros that we paid!".

It was not enough that the girl worked as a cleaner for some families in the town, nor was the work she did at home sufficient, Leda was forced to go out every day and beg for money.

Who knows what kind of financial return her greedy in-laws had in mind, who knows what they expected to earn, and for how long they thought the girl's existence in a state of slavery would last.

At every protest, at every refusal to beg (in fact, the girl had her dignity and was ashamed to stretch out her hand to passers-by in the street) the insults and the violence increased.

Leda suffered the dislocation of a shoulder and a broken arm. Then, with some money lent to her by a lady of S. Pietro Casale, where she used to go and clean, she fled to Puglia, but she was soon taken back to her husband.

Unfortunately, the painful story went on for several years; Leda meantime gave birth to three children. She moved to Switzerland with her husband and on her return to Piedmont she decided she couldn't carry on any longer. On the 19 December 2012, she reported everything to the police in Gravellona Toce.

Trials were held, and her husband and parents-in-law were sentenced. Leda was welcomed into a women's shelter; she was reassured and began to live her life without fear, beatings, or threats.

Subsequently, during the trial in the Court of Assizes in Ferrara, the girl showed she had pity for her husband. Many 'I don't remembers', lots of 'I don't knows', broke up the replies she gave to the investigators in court. Her reticence demonstrates generosity towards those who did her so much harm, and reveals her great love for her children, whom she considers her three jewels.

Leda was abused, segregated, wounded in body and soul, but cannot tell everything. She has pity for everyone. But they did not have it for a little girl, a slave, whose childhood was taken from her.

**Mariama, sold for 152 thousand euro! Goodbye studies. Goodbye dreams of a different life.**

Mariama was happy every time the teacher spoke words of approval and encouragement to her. She listened and saw a new world within her reach. The teacher's words were food for her spirit, the marks in her notebook were gems that enriched her miserable life. 'It won't always be like this, in these poor homes, with this life of hardship and very few things around me…'
She dreamt of a house full of books, a desk where she could write and study. She dreamt of educational trips and later a degree that would allow her to have an important profession.

Mariama's 13 years were lived day by day in an attempt to build a future, imagined and reflected in her dreamy eyes when she read about new subjects, learnt about the geographical composition of her country Niger, learnt that the world is big and wonderful. A world where children have the right to grow, study, play. A world where no one expects girls to be forced to marry strangers, unknown, old or decrepit adults.

Mariama knew about her family's extreme poverty. Her mother was a widow, with lots of children and lived a life of great sacrifice. 'Her life is tough - thought Mariama - but I'll be able to repay her when I work. Our existence will be made easier by the money I'll bring home, for her, my younger siblings. There'll come a time when we'll all live happily together'.


**The ambush**

One day, on her return from school, a neighbour warned her that someone was plotting against her. Someone with a lot of money, who knew how to convince others with money, offered Mariama's mother 152 thousand euro to buy her.
She was incredulous. It was an upheaval in her life. She told herself: "How is it possible? I'm one of the most studious pupils in my school. I'm top in mathematics. I've always told my mother I want to study, that I hate arranged marriages, that men who want to marry a little girl are disgusting! Why is this happening to me?".

Mariama saw her suitor and felt a strong sense of repulsion: she hated the idea of having sex with that man. She hated her life.

When they told her she no longer needed to go to school she was upset, devastated! She didn't sleep, she didn't eat. She didn't go out, after all what was the point of going out if she couldn't go to school.
Her companions laughed at her; the older women tried to convince her not to fight her fate.
They told her a woman must marry while she is still a virgin, so as soon as she is an adolescent, before someone takes advantage of her virginity and destroys what makes a girl attractive in the eyes of men.

Luckily, Mariama's story came to the knowledge of the humanitarian organisation *Plan International*, which at this point intervened and put every legal and logistical action into practice to restore the girl's right to go to school and refuse an early forced child marriage.

Mariama's mother, when charged, defended herself by asserting she did not know what to feed her children, the money was also for Mariama's home, and that basically she regretted having sold her thirteen-year-old daughter.
As always, there is conflict in the existence of poor families, between affection for their daughters and an enticing financial proposal in case of child marriage. The greatest conflict, however, is between progress and being tied to tribal customs, superstitions and fears.

Social workers must act to obtain results, as well as by resorting to the law, where it is even possible, with persuasive talk and encouragement towards change.

The effects of the intervention of *Plan International* were encouraging for Mariama's future, for the change the girl wanted. She clung to the hope that everything would go back to being like it was before, that the nightmare of an absurd marriage to an unknown adult would end.

And finally one morning the girl saw her dream come true. With her books under her arm she crossed the threshold of the door to her school, her eyes shining with happiness.

Since that day Mariama has studied and attended lessons with enthusiasm. She feels like another person. The child-bride is far from her daily life, a picture of suffering to be forgotten. "I'm Mariama - she tells herself - I have my whole life before me. I'll get a degree, I'll become a judge and I will be the protagonist of my existence."

## Sonita Alizadeh, a turning point in her life: music

Maria Sordino writes about her on "2anews.it":

*"Sonita Alizadeh is an activist, a rapper, an Afghan girl. She sings to denounce the injustices that women in her country suffer and hopes to be able to change their lot. Sonita said no to her fate as a child bride rapping her refusal: her song went viral two years ago".* [17]

The strength with which Sonita tried to escape the prospect of life as an outcast is admirable.
Born in Afghanistan, she lived in Iran, and immediately realised that life in the refugee camp where she lived with her family, was not the worst thing that could happen to her. She knew worse would happen when her father agreed to sell her for 9 thousand dollars to the man who offered that sum to marry her when she was still a child.

Intelligent and creative, young Sonita felt compassion for her mother, who had in turn been forced to be a child bride, and harboured rebellion against this state of things as she worked, and composed a piece of rap music *Dokhtar Forooshi (Daughters for sale).*
She played her piece to a filmmaker who decided to help her by recording her as she sang. The video was posted on the web and became an immediate

success, because it opened an identification process for all the girls forced to suffer abuse from a very young age.

*"Let me whisper to you my words, so no one hears that I speak of the selling of girls".*

**But let's look at the details of Sonita's story**

She first risked being sold as a bride at ten years old, in the city of Herat, where she lived with her parents. She was saved from this fate by the advance of the Taliban which forced her family to flee to Iran and there she learnt to read and write, although as an illegal immigrant because she couldn't go to school.
She began hanging out at the international organisation *Brides for sale,* and learnt to rap there through the young people she met.
At this point the deal to sell her for 9 thousand dollars comes into play. This is the sum a suitor offered her father.
In the meantime Sonita had met the Iranian filmmaker Rokhsareh Ghaem Maghami who liked the young girl's talent and became her friend.

To help her, Maghami convinced Sonita's parents to agree to a break - before marrying off their daughter - and accept 2 thousand dollars that she could offer for urgent expenses.

Then she helped the girl to record a "hymn to peace" and a song in favour of democratic elections in Afghanistan. The lyrics were the work of Sonita who had an aptitude for writing, to the point that she became so popular with government institutions that she overcame the ban that forbids women from making music in Iran.

But after this first step Sonita switched to her real fight. She sang the words that were dear to her heart. She appeared in a white dress, with a swollen and wounded face and sang on the web in Persian. In the video, wearing a wedding dress, the girl tells her story in a very long, poignant song directed at her father.

At first the words are barely whispered, to demonstrate the fear women have to speak out because of the impositions of Sharia law:

*"Let me whisper to you my words,*
*so no one hears that I speak of the selling of girls..*
*My voice shouldn't be heard, as it is against Sharia...*
*Women must remain silent. This is this city's tradition.*
*I scream to make up for a woman's lifetime silence.*
*I scream on behalf of the deep wounds on my body.*
*I scream for a body exhausted in its cage.*
*A body that broke under the price tags you put on it.*

*I am fifteen years old, from Herat.*
*[...]*
*Now, my father is concerned about the cost of life.*
*Whoever pays more the girl is his.*
*If I knew that you would keep count of my costs,*
*If I knew that you would keep track of my bites,*
*I would have returned hungry from the table, or I would have eaten your leftovers.*

*Like all other girls, I am caged.*
*I am seen as a sheep grown only to be devoured.*
*They repeat that it is time to sell me.*
*I am a person too, these are my eyes and ears.*
*Have you ever seen a sheep complaining about death?*
*Have you ever seen a sheep, as emotional as I am?*
*[...]*
*I hope that God will keep your smiles*
*And my smile, I will exchange with your pain.*
*But I wish you would review the Quran.*
*I wish you knew it doesn't say women are for sale.*
*Hold on, I need some peace.*
*Leave me alone. I am sick of the makeup.*
*My bruised face will not heal with makeup.*
*What you did to me, infidels won't do to Muslims.*

*[...]*
*I am leaving, but just in case you miss me,*
*I leave my doll here for you.*

*Don't let her cry like me.*
*Don't sell her, let her be a gift to remember me*
*by".*[18]


The song, of which I have only transcribed parts, went viral on the web and with the help of *Brides for Sale,*[19] went all around the world. The progress of Sonita Alizadeh's initiative can be measured by the large number of shares on the net by all those who, like her, dream of emancipation and growing up as free people.


Sonita's aims were to be able to study at University and build herself a future as an independent woman.
The girl supported by the association the *Strongherat Group,* also founded an association of her own *Sonita's dream,* with the aim of supporting poor families to convince them not to sell their girls as brides.
She also continued singing at musical concerts that reach the hearts of the people that listen better than any other initiative.


Her relationship with her parents also improved with time and mutual understanding.
The girl feared her father and her family might react badly when they listened to the words of the video. Instead the suffering and sincerity with which Sonita had spoken out even thrilled her parents, who thinking back to the mistake they

were making, reassured their daughter saying: "We'll never ask you to get married again!"
If one day, after she has achieved all her plans, she meets the right person, then they will be happy to bless her marriage with a man who makes her happy.

Nowadays, Sonita is very busy with her studies, her social activity, seeing her friends and participating in events.
She's grateful to the people who helped her, and today has thoughts of gratitude towards her family as well:

> *"It means a lot to know that my family went against our traditions for me. Now - she says smiling - I'm in a place I never imagined I'd get to".*

## When suffering gives you the strength to fight: Anika, the activist defending child brides

Anika is a beautiful Indian girl from Calcutta.
Having always lived in poverty, at 12 years old she was abandoned by her mother and remained alone with her sister Rajasthan.
The two little girls, at the wishes of their father, stopped going to school and started doing the housework. So they became part of the high statistical number of cases of school desertion that in developing countries counts 15 million girls; all

deprived of their right to an education, together with the natural one, of being able to live a carefree life suitable for childhood.

Despite everything Anika did not give up, she talked to her father, defended her rights, defended her sister; both of them wanted to go to school. But her father ignored the sisters' requests.
One day, thanks to a neighbour who went with them, they managed to contact *Save the Children*. The kind assistants at the association listened to them, promised to talk to their father, and after many arguments managed to convince the man to send his daughters back to school.

But all this was not enough for Anika. Although only twelve years old, she had a very high sense of duty towards those who do not receive any opportunities for cultural and social growth. She became an activist and fought - with a group of children - for the rights of little girls, and to prevent early and forced child marriage.

Anika had a method, a strategy that began as soon as she became aware that a family was about to plan a wedding: she intervened immediately. Together with her group she went to the parents of the future child bride and explained all the dangers to them that girls who marry and give birth as children face.

The girl often succeeded in her purpose and was really happy when she went to school with her friends who had been saved from a horrible existence, lived without rights and in absolute obedience to their husband and master; because that's what happens when a girl who should be playing games enters a house as the child wife of a man forced upon her by her family, never wanted, nor chosen, nor loved.

Even nowadays, patriarchy still hands down a system of oppression which considers women, especially little girls, beings who belong to the head of the family, who can for convenience, receive money, a dowry or some other benefit, by giving away a daughter in marriage.

The husband is almost always a stranger who intimidates his child wife; a brute from whom the unfortunate child would like to flee; and since most of the time she cannot escape that bitter fate, she soon realises that her so-called husband is a master who ends her every freedom; he's an adult who could be her father or grandfather and expects to have sex with her.

It's no use crying and screaming, pleading and protesting. Her despair has no effect. The man boasts ownership rights for having bought the girl as if she were an object, and he treats her like an object when he performs real acts of sexual abuse on her.

**Kriti Bharti, the 29-year-old who has blocked more than 900 child marriages**

Like Anika, Kriti Bharti is also to be admired for her civil commitment in defence of young girls.

We are still talking about India, about the northern state of Rajasthan; Kriti is only 29 years old, but she has achieved something truly commendable: she has prevented more than 900 little girls having the unhappy fate of marrying in childhood.

A joyful smile, a determined and optimistic nature characterise the beautiful Kriti, even though she had a difficult childhood, one of poverty, abandoned by her father at birth; of bitterness at having to leave school because of a poisoning that debilitated her and forced her to undergo treatment for a long time.

Yet there was always a light at the end of the tunnel for the girl who as soon as she could resumed her studies, she graduated and earned a doctorate in psychology.

Then Kriti started a social organisation "Saarthi Trust", of which she is designated President, its purpose being to help little girls and protect their rights to live their childhood, to study, to decide for themselves.

Supported by the government, the association has consulting help desks, school and family involvement projects, in order to make people understand the damage done by child marriage.

Where cultural persuasion is not effective the team takes legal action to have marriages annulled, and to date Kriti has saved more than 6,000 children and more than 5 thousand women, with legal assistance, and a rehabilitation project to lift them out of social exclusion, helping them to resume their studies, learn a craft, look towards the future with optimism.


**Parul, the champion that nobody wanted**

People are not born champions but they become them. Some may be born instead with a disability, which in certain rural areas may induce people to consider someone who does not have the full efficiency of their functions as a reject.
We are in Bangladesh, Parul was born with a mild cognitive disability. What can we do? Her relatives thought.
They resigned themselves and carried on giving her as little care as possible, while her brother, healthy and promising, received lots of attention and affection; starting with their food, his was better and much more than Parul was given.
The disparity between the two children was such that the little girl lost weight and practically abandoned to her own devices, developed severe malnutrition.

But a star lit up in the sky for Parul on the evening the little girl was noticed by the activists of the organisation *Bangladesh Protibondhi Foundation,* who immediately realised how she was being discriminated against because of her disability.

The family considered it unnecessary to send her to school, her friends teased her, and based on a kind of retrograde mindset, the people of her town thought it was all her mother's fault for having given birth to a child with problems.

To deal with the serious criminalisation of Parul's rights, the assistants of the *Bangladesh Protibondhi Foundation* began a long job of persuasion on the family, explaining human rights, financial aid and giving them an introduction into social development itineraries.

The change of mentality was difficult, but slowly it happened like a drop that wears away a stone. The words of the kind mediators convinced the parents to send the girl back to school.

So the star that lit up the little girl's life, continued to shine for her, and after a while an incredible surprise happened! Parul, having gone back to school, showed a remarkable talent in sports. She swam well and she loved being in the water.

She trained and became better each day; she was accepted for sports competitions including international ones and she won: medals, awards and even the gold medal at the Special Olympic Games in Australia in 2013, and then in the United States.

Her country, her father and her mother are proud of her achievements, and they look back with shame on the times when the little girl was pushed aside into a corner like a category B person. They regret their behaviour and fear that a lifetime will perhaps not suffice to overcome the remorse they feel.


**Aisha, they said she was possessed by demons**

Just how many anti-feminist yarns can you spin if you're a misogynist? Aisha's uncle invented an enormous one: he said the girl was possessed by demons.

The story began in Togo, Africa, when Aisha, having been orphaned by her father and following her mother's flight, was placed in the care of an uncle who welcomed her but considered her nothing more than another mouth to feed.
So he couldn't wait to marry her off to someone and a daily procession of men began: adults for the most part ugly paedophiles, all very tenacious in their attempt to gain Aisha's hand from her uncle.

The uncle for his part insisted and urged the child: "You must choose one!"
The girl refused. He repeated the same thing several times a day:

"You have to get married. You can't stay in my house. You have to go to a husband. That's how we do things!"

But Aisha's ruthless relative could not win, because she managed to contact *Plan International,* where the operators took an interest in her case, and listening to her teachers at school, found out that Aisha had a brilliant mind and a great deal of willingness to learn.

The organisation decided to arrange practical help for the girl, but in the meantime her fight against her uncle's wishes was not on an equal footing. Aisha suffered and did all she could not to give in to the man's orders.
The incredible case of the girl - forced to marry despite being a bright and intelligent student - was described in an article by Valeria Panzeri on "Urban Post", where moving phrases of sorrow mixed with hope appeared:

*"I want to study; I don't want to be a wife to anybody. I ran away from hell, when my father died, I hadn't realised that the real hell is now. My brother can study, but there's not enough money for us both, so they've decided to invest in him because he's a boy. But I'm clever, ask my teachers, I can do just as well or even better than the boys".*[20]

Her uncle, who stubbornly intended to impose his

will on the girl, at a certain point invented a theory according to which his niece was acting so resolutely because she was possessed by demons. And to prove that the nonsense he was talking was true he added that the backache Aisha suffered was the work of the devil.

So a new form of possession of the bodies of innocent little girls was born; according to this immoral theory it is inconceivable that the body of a little girl should remain intact and free from misappropriation. Wherever there is a firm refusal to be abused by an adult man, the devil himself will wreak havoc in the little girl's body; occupying it, causing her back pain.

So there is no escape for a poor girl who just wants to grow, study and in her free time perhaps even play a little. The choice is between an old paedophile or the devil.


**Outcast Aisha**

Outcast and considered cursed Aisha's uncle entrusted her
to a religious who undertook her 'redemption'.

*"The priest is treating me - wrote the girl - because he says my backache is only the consequence of my wrong behaviour; I must do what he orders me to do, then perhaps I'll get better"*.

How long would this little girl resist against so much inappropriate meddling? The priest, her uncle, her relatives, and now also a religious. She was alone against an unbearable swarm of advice, threats, promises; intrusions by people that it is hard to believe could be in good faith in wanting so stubbornly to override the wish of a little girl to remain a child.

In addition to the persuasive actions of all her relatives, there was the daily appearance of a man who continually tried to undermine her purity: with gifts, money, clumsy attention. Aisha did not accept even a penny from this other pervert and just studied, studied, studied. She kept her backache and studied. She cried in secret and studied. She wanted to get her diploma. She wanted a different future, far from this riff raff. A place where girls can look to the future and see the sun on the horizon. Let's hope Aisha finds the right legal protection of her human rights and to fight legalised paedophilia.
We're rooting for her.


## Onur a photographer with a soul who opposed the marriage of a child

Onur Albayrak is a professional Turkish photographer, specialising in ceremonies. He was called out to a wedding. He agreed his services, the price and the place to go and take the pictures.

The wedding was in Malatya, in eastern Anatolia. Once there Onur realised that the bride was 15 years old, trembling and terrified.
The young girl, as well as being forced, was not the right age for marriage as prescribed by current law.
The photographer refused to continue his work and told the bridegroom and guests this, very clearly. Chaos ensued. The bridegroom was furious, the relatives remonstrated with Onur, who remained firm about his decision not to take any photographs. A fight broke out, but among the general disappointment Onur left.
For nothing in the world was he going to become an accomplice to an injustice:

*"I am happy to have contributed to raising public awareness about this problem -* Onur Albayrak explained to the Daily News *- Over the past two days my phone has not stopped ringing. The groom came to my studio about two weeks before the date of the wedding, but he was alone. I saw the bride for the first time at the wedding, she was a child and I felt her fear, she was trembling. I decided to take a stand"*.[21]
The photographer's gesture brought the phenomenon of child marriage in Turkey back to the centre of the debate and thanks to social media it entered the public domain.
Albayrak has become a real hero, imitated as well by many other photographers who have told him they intend to follow the same course every time they find themselves at a forced child marriage.

This is an example of how it's possible, with a simple refusal, to form opinions and change things despite the displeasure of the religious fundamentalists who are leading the country backwards in time and trampling on Turkish law, as well as the rights of children to live their childhood.


## A radio to put an end to child marriage

In the Democratic Republic of the Congo the population lives in extreme poverty. There is a sort of isolation from the rest of the world: no Internet connection, no television, no publications.
The only opportunity of information and knowledge is the radio, which as it is listened to a lot is a powerful means of dissemination, not only for entertainment and listening to music, but as an element of criticism and social awareness.

Photo: Radio Ondese

Among the various broadcasters Radio Ondese affiliated to *Girls Not Brides*, transmits in South

Kivu for 11 hours a day to over 30,000 listeners, with lots of programmes that explain the negative impact of child marriage on society.

The stories and interviews follow one after the other with the listeners' involvement, and the organisation of workshops and listening groups. This daily work, has a sure reflection of cultural growth on the population, and gains new audiences who are passionate about the stories broadcast in FM.


## THE STORIES TOLD ON THE RADIO


**Salama forced to marry the father of her son**

*"I didn't want to marry him even if I was pregnant. He'd betrayed me, he didn't have a job."*

These are the words of a 15-year-old girl forced to marry and live with her in-laws, where, after the birth of her child, she saw the problems in her miserable life worsen.

Hers was a daily life of hardship. The little money the girl received from the family soon ran out.

She's called Salama. She conceived a baby without realising, then everything happened quickly. Marriage, the hateful duties, including having to succumb to her husband.

Her mother-in-law didn't help the ménage, she seemed to barely tolerate her, with little grace and lots of reprimands.

The girl became sad. Some days she ate nothing, she cried without being able to explain her pain. She knew that speaking out was no use where the rules are against the lives of girls. She kept quiet because she saw no possibility of getting out of what she considered a prison.

She fell ill, she felt weak and painful, but there was no possibility of either a medical consultation, or of buying medicine. Exhausted, Salama asked her mother to let her go back home, but she refused.

Many days of difficult conditions of survival went by, until the activists of Women for Equal Chances (WEC), associated with *Girls Not Brides* went to the local church to speak about child marriage. Salama approached them, she told them about her poverty and despair; she asked them to go and speak to her mother and her whole family to convince them to let her return home. Which the activists did, and her mother, already made aware of the consequences of child marriage by listening to the radio programme, listened to the words of the association's envoys and agreed to let her daughter return home.

*The WEC organisation works with the communities of the DRC to raise awareness about the damage of child marriage and change the community's beliefs. Photo credit: WEC.*

After the positive change in her existence, Salama appears to be reborn, she is happy to be able to help other girls and make them all aware that there is the possibility to live a life, where you plan to go to school, and choose what you want to make of your own life. She tells her story during the WEC radio programmes, to inform communities that are listening about the social, human and financial damage of child marriage.

Like her, many other girls collaborate with the radio to tell their stories, invite the people to participate in the common fight against child marriage.

The radio is confirmed to be a powerful means of dissemination and diffusion, because people with little education, of all ages, by listening to the

transmissions are able to understand the error that occurs when you force little girls to marry too young.
This way, little by little, the path of cultural growth and change towards the progress of the rural population is completed.

Thanks to the network_Population Media Centre (PMC), which is a member of the *Girls Not Brides* organisation, effective programs for social emancipation are produced and broadcast all over Africa.
Surveys on the effects of listening to the radio published by *Girls Not Brides* give the following results:

*"In Nigeria, listeners of the PMC show "Ruwan Dare" are twice as likely to be convinced that a woman should marry after age 19 compared to non-listeners. In Senegal, listeners of "Ngelawu Nawet" are convinced that a woman should be at least 18 years old before marriage. Whilst in Niger, "Gobe da Haske" has induced radio-listeners to support girls having to wait until they are at least 20 years old before accepting to marry".*

**A betrothed child bride, in super modern Milan. Her mother objected**

The trip was already organised. The tickets for the journey from Italy to Bangladesh were already booked. The little girl, who we'll call Amina to safeguard her right to privacy, was ten-years-old. Her father was convinced he had to marry her off to a twenty-two-year-old relative.
Did he ask for her mother's opinion? No. Nor was he concerned about how the child might be disturbed by these indecent proposals.

The story was reported by the newspaper '*Il Giorno*'.
The facts took place in Milan, where the family lived. Little Amina was segregated at home. She was not allowed to go to school, or read anything, if not the Quran.
Her father was almost a stranger to Amina who was already nine years old when, after a very long absence that seemed to have lasted forever, he returned to Bangladesh to take her to Italy with her mother Farah.

In Milan, mother and child lived segregated at home; everything was forbidden; school, friendships, entertainment.
There were no prerogatives for growth, no life plans. The father's only aim was a marriage between his daughter and a 22-year-old relative who lived in their country. But for that to happen,

the child had to go back to Bangladesh. But then how difficult was that? He just had to buy the tickets and go.

But Mama Farah didn't agree. She didn't want her daughter to end up like her. She had been forced into marriage at a very young age with a man she did not know and did not love. And just look at how it had turned out! A life of segregation, with no consideration or affection. In practice her daughter and her life with a sort of stranger.

Farah who had been unable to refuse when she was forced to marry, defended her daughter this time.

She argued with her husband every day; she told him she didn't intend to make the child marry, she absolutely did not want to make her go back to Bangladesh, that the little girl was entitled to go to school, and one day choose the husband she wanted, if she wanted a husband.

Daily quarrels, abuse and insults ensued. The man went as far as threatening his wife with a knife. He was determined to achieve the result he'd promised his relative. Give him the child in marriage.

Seeing the imminent danger, Farah did the only thing possible to stop the abuse. She tore up their passports. The man flew into a rage. The shouting and blows increased. Amina cried, she was frightened and upset by the
hostile atmosphere in the family, the abuse her mother suffered and above all because she hated

the relative who wanted to take her childhood away from her.

Her father, resolute in his intentions, went to report the theft of their passports and get new ones. He had decided to marry off his daughter and that was that!
Then, Farah reported him. For everything: the abuse, the intent to make their child marry, the threats, the segregation.

The police and the judiciary began proceedings against her husband, father and master. The trial is currently ongoing with lots of accusations. The man denies everything, but it will be difficult to go on denying things when faced with witness statements and proof.
Farah and Amina have been welcomed into an association against violence and live in a safe house. They are following an educational programme with the aim of integration into social and working life for the mother and education for the daughter.
Finally, they are starting to feel calmer and happier. Perhaps they have escaped hell.

## Noura, Condemned to Death

It was with great joy that we received the news that Noura Hussein is safe. The woman risked the death sentence by hanging, but over a million people all over the world signed the petition to support her release.

The appeal by the 'Italians for Darfur' organisation and the dissemination of the case through the press, created international interest; pressure mounted, publications on the net, statements by famous people multiplied, until the Court of Appeals of Omdurman, in Sudan, converted her death sentence to five years in prison, plus a penalty of 12 thousand dollars.

Noura's is the story of a child bride aged 16, who could not bear having an unpleasant and overbearing man next to her. She refused to have sexual relations but her cries of pain did not stop the man who considered himself the owner of her body. Until her disgust and desperation overwhelmed Noura who, during yet another attempt to rape her  by her husband, killed him.

Sudanese law allows marriage from the age of ten, and therefore, considering her husband to have the right to abuse her, condemned Noura Hussein to hang.

A worldwide campaign *#JusticeForNoura* was immediately started for the girl who had been in prison since May 2017.
Besides *Italians for Darfur, Amnesty International,* and three United Nations agencies also take action on her behalf and write to the Sudanese president Omar al Bashir to ask him to pardon her.
After this initial result which forestalled her death sentence, the girl's lawyers continued the legal battle to have her declared innocent.

# MALALA YOUSAFZAI
# RECEIVES THE SACHAROV PRIZE

***The drama of child marriage is not just about human suffering, here's how it weighs on the global economy***

The drama of the little girls whose childhood is stolen from them upsets sensitive souls and seems to leave entire pockets of the third world population indifferent, almost accustomed to this barbarism; just as it seems to leave the political world indifferent which is very slow to take action and adopt measures to prevent child marriage.

There are more or less seven hundred million children in the world who are forced into marriage in regions such as sub-Saharan Africa, South Asia and India. Among the countries with the highest average of child brides are Chad, Mali, Guinea and Burkina Faso. But it seems that nowhere is untouched by it. Children are forced to marry both in civilised Europe and in the great and modern America. In Italy as in London, in Romania as in Belgium. The "young brides" returning from their countries of origin, having been sent there on holiday and forced to marry an old man, or in any case a man twice their age, are many, and to add insult to deception the newly married husband may even be given the right to request a residence permit in the country where the abused little girl lives.

The information that the phenomenon of child marriage, in addition to being immoral, also creates serious economic losses, appears to be little valued in the political world.
A study supported by the World Bank and the International Research Centre on child brides, reports that to compensate for the damage caused to this segment of the young population, every state spends much more than what it could spend to stop it through targeted investments.

UNICEF confirms that every year 700 million minors are forced into marriage and consequently their full growth is interrupted, both physical and cultural.
Add to this the lack of education, school drop-outs, early pregnancies, the commitment of health services to treat numerous health issues such as premature childbirths and neonatal diseases, and it becomes obvious how high social negativity and spending to tackle the consequences really are.
Among the certified inauspicious outcomes of child marriage, an increase in poverty and a high incidence of pre-and post-partum mortality of both mother and child are among the most prominent.

According to the research mentioned above unless governments put an end to early marriages, in the decades to come billions of dollars will have to be spent in developing countries, to buffer the negative effects in the health care, cultural and productive sectors; consequently, global projects to eradicate poverty will be hampered.

The arithmetic is soon done. Girls who begin to have children at very early ages, raise the average per capita number of children, as well as increasing the number of poor families with little food available and almost no training to aspire to a sufficiently remunerative job.

In order to put a stop to this trend, it is important to ensure attendance at school, improve school education, expanding the opportunities of finding a well-paid job as a direct consequence of studying and learning.

The study by the International Research Centre on child brides foresees that in 2030, if the phenomenon can be blocked, economic benefits of ninety billion euro will be obtained. Due to the reasons already described, the reduction of illness, the reduction of the mortality rate, and the economic growth that follows every investment made in culture and education.

## Child Brides, the good fortune to go to school

People who lead a comfortable life, with enough food, education, entertainment, and various cultural options, do not imagine that for many little girls in developing countries the chance to go to school is considered a reason to feel immensely happy: an achievement that throws open the door to a better future.

According to UNESCO, 57 million children do not have access to primary school and, of them more than half, 30 million, are girls. Moreover, a good 65 million girls do not have access to any type of study, so many young girls are offered as brides to men who are often double, if not triple, their age.

In the developing countries, according to Onlus Plan, girls who are not allowed to study live in rural areas, are mostly poor and suffer discrimination from their youngest years of infancy.
They are only considered useful for housework; they live solitary lives and cannot attend either school or other social gatherings. The fear of the families is that every girl, before marrying, may lose the value of her virginity through abuse on any occasion, including even the simple fact of leaving the house to go to school or learn a trade.
So to avoid presumed possible abuse they commit the cruellest of errors with early marriage. Girls' rights are trampled on, their childhood snatched away from them as they are led by the hand towards the violence to be suffered from their so-called husband.

A child bride is a human being without defences, nor cultural tools, to avoid her cruel fate. She is left at the mercy of unfavourable events, such as the risk of

contagion of sexual diseases (including AIDS and HIV), high-risk pregnancies, miscarriages, postpartum haemorrhage and death.
According to figures released by the Plan Organisation (*Because I am a Girl 2012* Report), unless steps are taken to block marriages at an early age, by 2020 there will be 140 million child brides.


## THE NO MORE CHILD BRIDES PETITION


### *#Maipiùsposebambine*

In September 2013, with Onerpo and through the Avaaz.org portal, we started an online petition aimed at the governments of Niger, Chad, Mali, Nepal, India, Bangladesh, Mozambique, Nicaragua, Ethiopia, Yemen and more generally addressed to any country where the serious violation of the rights of little girls is tolerated.

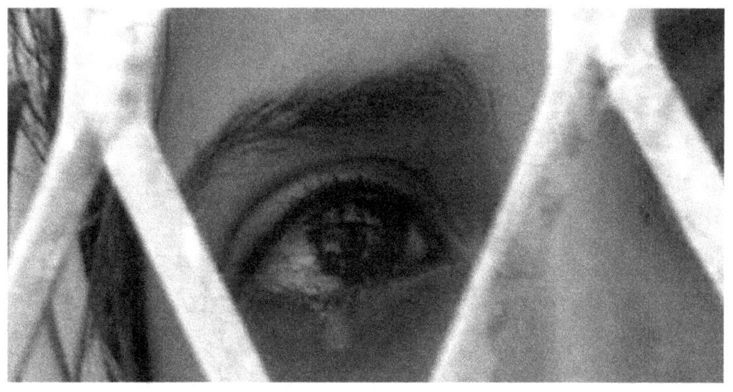

## The invitation-text to sign

*"Child brides sold as objects, with a rite of marriage or an exchange of goods and/or money, to people of adult age, suffer real abuse, an act which aids paedophilia. All this goes against the International Convention on the Rights of the Child because the Convention is against torture and any other form of cruel, inhuman or degrading treatment or punishment of children. The Convention prohibits harming the health of minors and sets forth in Article 3 that every decision, legislative action, legal measure, public or private initiative, must have as its primary consideration the greater interest of the child. This Convention was signed by 61 countries on the 26 January 1990 in New York, and is based on a series of human rights documents, including:*

*• The Charter of the United Nations of 1945;*
*• The Universal Declaration of Human Rights of 1948;*
*• the Geneva convention (1924).*

*According to the United Nations in the next ten years every day 25,000 girls will be forced to marry in the world. 100 million girls will marry before the age of 18.*
*The psychological effects are devastating for little girls torn from childhood, forced into marriage. The physical damage is serious: due to injuries, childbirth, or early pregnancies. Many little girls*

*are infected with AIDS, especially in Africa, by their adult, mature or old husbands".*[22]


## The signatures and the commitment on social media (*15 September 2013*)

The publication of the *#maipiùsposebambine* website and relevant Facebook page by the monitoring centre for the safeguarding of equal opportunities (Onerpo), generated considerable interest in Italian public opinion.

At global level, Onerpo became part of the "Girls Not Brides" organisation to participate in actions to fight early and forced marriage, together with another 400 organisations throughout the world, which over the years have grown to more than a thousand.

*Amnesty International* in turn started a campaign to fight the repugnant phenomenon which it gave the same slogan *#maipiùsposebambine,* disseminated through the web and the Italian *Corriere della Sera* newspaper.

Our Facebook page 'Mai più spose bambine' at first attracted moderate interest, and it seemed that the issue of child brides was seen as something to consider with detachment because it concerned countries that were far away from Italy and Europe. Then as the publication of interviews and stories told directly by the girls themselves continued, attention for the problem increased and, together with requests for information, signings of the petition also multiplied. Consequently, new blogs and web pages have been started with images, videos, the promotion of conferences at various institutional sites, and the involvement of parliamentary groups.


# CHILD, EARLY AND FORCED MARRIAGE IN EUROPE AT WHAT POINT IS THE SITUATION

*(Amnesty International Conference, Rome 4 March 2016)*


## A violation of human rights

Estimates of forced marriage (FM) in Europe are few and often discordant. In 2011 in the UK the government's Forced Marriage Unit (FMU) intervened in 1500 cases where unions were being celebrated without the willingness of both spouses; of these a good 56 involved people with mental disabilities.

According to some estimates, every year 8 thousand teenagers with British passports are forced to accept marriage against their will: 30% are children and 15% are less than 15 years old.

To remedy this situation, Britain has been discussing the introduction of a strict law, for some time now, that will make forced marriage become a criminal offence with a prison sentence for parents.

The first European country to ban forced marriage in its domestic legislation was Norway, through a specific criminal provision in 2003 (*Any person who by force, deprivation of liberty, improper pressure or any other unlawful conduct or by threats of such conduct forces anyone to enter into a marriage shall be guilty of causing a forced marriage*), which it subsequently completed in 2007 with the addition of civil and administrative provisions.

In Switzerland, the phenomenon of FM appears to be on the rise. A university study (University of Neuchatel) on behalf of the Federal Office for Migration (FOM) shows that from 2010 to 2012 about 350 women were forced to marry and 390 had to renounce having a relationship they had chosen freely. Whereas, another 660 was prevented from initiating divorce proceedings. These are women aged between 18 and 24 years old, from the Balkan countries, Turkey and Sri Lanka.
In Switzerland, a law on unions ratified using force is being approved, to be able to prosecute ex officio: anyone responsible can be sentenced to five years in prison.

It appears however that the phenomenon varies between European Union regions or countries. According to the survey carried out among EC Home Affairs Stakeholders in 2012, a number of European countries (CZ, LV, LT, PL, RO, SK) stated they had addressed issues related to the phenomenon of FM, while many others (AT, BE, BG, EE, FI, IT, LU, PT,

FR, RO) declared they did not have any information available on the phenomenon.

None of the EU member states has fielded a quantitative analysis of early and forced marriage. Only some NGOs like the Red Cross and *Terres des Femmes* have produced data, but it is mainly indicative information that does not provide an adequate picture of the phenomenon.
In the absence of official statistics, reference can be made to the 2013 *State of the World* Report produced by UNICEF, which gives the geographical areas and states where the practice of early or child marriage is in use.

In Italy, FM is rising with the increase in immigration of families from the Indian subcontinent and some Arab countries.
To date there is no official census of the data. It has recently been noted that, although forced marriage is a practice that is tolerated in various cultures, at a time when families are emigrating and trying to reproduce their own roots on host soil, the phenomenon undergoes a change from arranged marriage to "arranged forced" marriage, with coercive actions, threats, both physical and psychological violence: banishment, estrangement of the "disobedient" person, control, restrictions on the freedom of movement.

In December 2013, the Department for Equal Opportunities commissioned the [*Italian*] association

*Le Onde Onlus* to carry out a survey on the phenomenon to identify a target of victims and potential victims. However, the task proved to be complex and difficult to carry out due to stakeholders' refusal to cooperate in order to protect their own privacy, the difficulty of reporting members of the family or community, the absence of a certificate setting out the true age of the persons being examined.

The UNICEF mapping shows that amongst the communities in Italy most at risk of FM are the South East Asian countries (Bangladesh, Pakistan, India, Sri Lanka), characterised however by a limited presence of women; some African countries (Senegal, Ghana, Nigeria, Egypt) - apart from Nigeria - are also characterised by a low female presence. The female or male gender of immigrants is differentiated at regional level and the 'highest risk' communities are concentrated in some specific regions or areas. The most numerous communities in our country are from Morocco and Albania, with the presence even of second generation women.
More than half of the Moroccan nationals reside in Lombardy, Emilia Romagna and Piedmont. In Lombardy, Tuscany and Emilia Romagna almost half of the immigrant citizens are Albanians, while in Sicily most are native to North Africa.

Specific consideration should be given to the Roma, Sinti and Camminanti populations; reference to a qualitative survey conducted by the [*Italian*]

Fondazione Basso indicates the tradition of arranging marriages as a community and family strategy for them.

## The renowned cases of Hina and Kawor

Italian public opinion has started to become aware of the phenomenon of immigrant girls, regarding forced marriage, especially since 2006, after the case of Hina, a Pakistani girl living in the province of Brescia, killed by her father because she fell in love with an Italian; or Kawor, a young Indian girl who lived near Modena for several years, but having been widowed was forced to marry her husband's brother, and when he wanted to join her in Italy committed suicide by throwing herself under a train.

Among the European resolutions, the text of the resolution of the Parliamentary Assembly of the Council of Europe recalls that all Member States have ratified the 1989 United Nations Convention on the Rights of the Child, and that sexual abuse of children constitutes a serious violation of these rights. It also recalls that, under Directive 2011/92/EU, anyone who engages in sexual activity with a child who has not attained the age of sexual consent shall be punishable by a custodial sentence of at least five years. Incitement and abetting are also punishable, as well as abuse of a recognised position of trust or authority.

## More on the laws in Italy

Under Italian law vitiated consent is a cause for annulment of marriage. The Civil Code provides that marriage can only be entered into by persons who have the requirements of age, ability to understand and discern, and are free from the constraints of previous marriages.

In the international arena, Italy co-chaired negotiations to define the text of a UN Resolution with Sierra Leone, which reiterates that early and forced marriages represent a violation of human rights, in particular of women and girls. The resolution stresses the importance of involving all of society and calls on the stakeholders involved in the humanitarian sector to strengthen monitoring and prevention measures to combat recourse to early and forced marriages.

The active role played by Italy to eliminate early and forced marriage, as well as female genital mutilation, is proof yet again of the priority given, by the Ministry of Foreign Affairs and International Cooperation, to the rights of children, especially girls. Our country has been a member since 2013 of the cross-regional group of countries that deal with these issues, and on the 16 July 2015 our Parliament approved the motion - first signing by Pia Locatelli - concerning 'initiatives in the international sphere related to the phenomenon of early and forced child marriage'.

Earlier, Italy had ratified the Istanbul Convention on the 27 June 2013 (Law no. 77). Additionally, FM is mentioned in paragraph 18 of the Ministerial Decree concerning the 'Charter of Values of Citizenship and Integration' (2007) and in some regional laws, in particular the Molise region's recent laws on gender-based violence (R.L. no. 15/2013, Article 1, and Lombardy's R.L. no. 11/2012, Article 1).

## The violation of the human rights of women and girls

For the purposes of recognising a marriage celebrated in another country, the Italian authorities cannot verify the existence of the consent of both spouses in a marriage that takes place outside Italy. Whilst that consent is necessary if the marriage takes place in Italy. The result is that the families of young women living in Italy take the girls back to their countries of origin, to have the marriage recognised on their daughter's return to Italy. The absence of any form of control makes it difficult to identify forced marriages and protect women who have been subjected to them.

One of the obstacles in analysing the phenomenon is that many early marriages are not official and are not registered nor picked up by any of the normal statistical systems. There is very little national data on marriages under 14 years of age, and still less on those under the age of 10.

## Gender inequality originates violence

The phenomenon of forced and early marriage reflects that of violence against women which increases in brutality when it involves girls whose childhood, dreams, and future are taken away from them.
The main factor that determines this abuse is gender inequality that assigns women a lesser role than men. From these conditions of inequality derive the numerous forms of patriarchal control over the sexuality and reproductive life of women and to which marriage practices that violate their freedom can also be traced.

Certain forms of obligation to submit to arranged marriages and control over women's sexuality were carried out in Italy, until awareness of women's rights by the women themselves brought about a social and legal change.

## The case of Franca Viola in Italy

A case that caused a stir in the sixties was that of Franca Viola, a 17-year-old from Alcamo who, in 1965, refused to marry her kidnapper, Filippo Melodia, who belonged to a Mafia family.
At that time, in accordance with Article 544 of the criminal code, there was the possibility to extinguish the offence of rape, including to the detriment of a minor, if it was followed by a so-called 'shotgun

wedding'. Franca Viola refused to get married and her kidnapper was arrested and sentenced to 11 years in prison. The girl became a symbol of freedom for many women in Sicily and throughout Italy.

Rape, until then considered a crime against morality, became a crime 'against the person' several years later, when on the 15 February 1996 the Italian Parliament approved Law no. 66, on the first signing by Tina Lagostena Bassi, a member of parliament and chair of the National Commission for Equality and Equal Opportunities between men and women, at the Presidency of the Council of Ministers.


## Cross-culturalism, rights, and lack of culture

Acceptance and the subject of cross-culturalism are encompassing of people's rights, not exclusionary. There can no excuse, either historical, or anthropological, or religious, for justifying an action of real sexual abuse against girls as 'a fact of culture'. The culture of hosted populations is often used as a pretext to hide an inability to act against violent actions, but a crime cannot be justified as a cultural factor, just as a cannibal cannot be allowed to eat his own kind.
Rather, culture should be considered in the positive sense of the word that indicates "a body of knowledge that concurs to form and refine the personality or totality of the literary, scientific,

artistic knowledge and social institutions and policies of a whole people".

Conversely, however much the actions are prevaricating, discriminatory, cruel; when they restrict freedoms and individual rights we must use the right definition and say that it's not about culture but "lack of culture" that takes steps backwards towards barbarism, violence and crime.

Culture is dissemination of positive concepts and for the improvement of humankind, it can be the lever to dissuade, deter and forever abolish the phenomenon of child brides.[23]

# Table A: UNICEF 20 countries with the highest prevalence of child marriage in the world (%)

Tabella A: UNICEF 20 Paesi con la più alta prevalenza di Matrimoni precoci nel mondo (%)
Popolazioni in Italia

| Paese | Residenti in Italia | | Matrimonio prima dei 15 anni | Matrimonio prima dei 18 anni |
|---|---|---|---|---|
| | M | F | | |
| Niger | 32.675 | 33.956 | 16% | 75% |
| Centrafricana Rep | 79 | 59 | 29% | 68% |
| Ciad | 568 | 120 | 29% | 68% |
| Bangladesh | 80.106 | 33.705 | 32% | 66% |
| Guinea | 3.106 | 1.581 | 20% | 63% |
| Mozambico | 164 | 237 | 21% | 56% |
| Mali | 3.697 | 539 | 15% | 55% |
| Sud Sudan | 6 | 1 | 9% | 52% |
| Burkina Faso | 10.287 | 5.375 | 10% | 52% |
| Malawi | 32 | 32 | 12% | 50% |
| Madagascar | 412 | 989 | 14% | 48% |
| India | 93.872 | 56.590 | 18% | 47% |
| Eritrea | 5.830 | 5.663 | 20% | 47% |
| Somalia | 5.591 | 3.077 | 8% | 45% |
| Sierra Leone | 811 | 578 | 44% | 18% |
| Zambia | 140 | 134 | 9% | 42% |
| Etiopia | 3.535 | 5.885 | 16% | 41% |
| Nicaragua | 192 | 448 | 10% | 41% |
| Nepal | 775 | 448 | 10% | 41% |
| Domenicana rep | 10.219 | 18.908 | 12% | 41% |

# Table B: non-EU citizens resident in Italy on 01.01.2013 and UNICEF percentage of child marriage

Tabella B: cittadini non-EU residenti in Italia al 01/01/2013 e % UNICEF Matrimoni Precoci[9]

| Paese | M | F | TOT | Matrimonio prima dei 18 anni | Matrimonio prima dei 15 anni |
|---|---|---|---|---|---|
| Marocco | 288.242 | 225.132 | 513.374 | 16% | 3% |
| Albania | 261.632 | 236.129 | 497.761 | 10% | 1% |
| Cina Rep. Popolare | 155.800 | 148.968 | 304.768 | | |
| Ucraina | 45.325 | 179.263 | 224.588 | 10% | 1% |
| Filippine | 66.838 | 91.470 | 158.308 | 14% | 2% |
| India | 93.872 | 56.590 | 150.462 | 18% | 47% |
| Moldova | 49.333 | 99.898 | 149.231 | | |
| Egitto | 87.592 | 35.937 | 123.529 | 17% | 2% |
| Tunisia | 77.525 | 43.958 | 121.483 | | |
| Bangladesh | 80.106 | 33.705 | 113.811 | 32% | 66% |
| Peru' | 43.578 | 65.796 | 109.374 | 19% | 35% |
| Serbia/Kosovo/ Montenegro | 57.401 | 49.097 | 106.498 | | |
| Sri Lanka | 54.984 | 43.695 | 98.679 | 12% | 2% |
| Pakistan | 65.595 | 32.326 | 97.921 | 24% | 7% |
| Senegal | 68.401 | 23.970 | 92.371 | 33% | 12% |
| Ecuador | 37.162 | 53.138 | 90.300 | 22% | 4% |
| Macedonia ex Rep. Jugoslava | 46.077 | 37.371 | 83.448 | 7% | 1% |
| Nigeria | 32.675 | 33.956 | 66.631 | 16% | 75% |
| Ghana | 33.452 | 22.569 | 56.021 | 21% | 5% |
| Brasile | 12.321 | 34.643 | 46.964 | 36% | 11% |

# SOURCES – BIBLIOGRAPHY


- *Council of Europe and the role of National Human Rights Institutions, Equality bodies and Ombudsman offices in promoting equality and social inclusion;*
- *To the Human Rights Council, within its Universal Periodic Review, for consideration at the 20th session;*
- *RAPVITE ricerca azione partecipata sulle vittime della tratta di esseri umani, dei crimini d'onore e dei matrimoni forzati in seno alle comunità immigrate africane e dell'Europa dell'Est [participatory action research on the victims of human trafficking, honour crimes and forced marriages within African and Eastern European immigrant communities];*
- *ERRC (European Roma Rights Centre), Idea Rom, Opera Nomadi, Parallel submission to the Committee on the Elimination of all forms of Discrimination Against Women on Italy under Article 18 of the Convention;*
- *Trajectoires et origines, Enquête sur la diversité des populations en Francesous la direction de Cris Beauchemin, Christelle Hamel et Patrick Simon;*
- *Girls Not Brides, Global partnership of more than 1000 civil society organisations committed to ending child marriage;*
- *The Elders, international non-governmental organisation of public figures noted as elder statesmen, peace activists, and human rights advocates, who were brought together by Nelson Mandela in 2007;*
- *Women for Afghan Women (WAW) Humanitarian organization for the rights of Afghan girls;*
- *ONERPO - National and European monitoring centre for the safeguarding of equal opportunities;*
- *European Convention on Human Rights (ECHR) 1950;*
- *[Italian] LAW no. 66 of 15 February 1996, law against sexual violence;*
- *Charter of Fundamental Rights of the European Union (CFR) of 2000;*
- *Decree of the Ministry of the Interior, 23 April 2007, "Charter of Values of Citizenship and Integration";*
- *Shadow report, prepared by the Italian platform "Work in progress: 30 years of CEDAW, Convention on the Elimination of All Forms of Discrimination against Women", June 2011;*

- *Bill proposed by Giulia Bongiorno on forced marriage, 21 Nov. 2012;*
- *Istanbul Convention: Law no. 77 of 27 June 2013 (in the [Italian] Off. Gazette 1st July 2013, no. 152) "Ratification and implementation of the Council of Europe Convention on preventing and combating violence against women and domestic violence, opened on 11 May 2011 in Istanbul;*
- *Annual Report 2013 of the United Nations Population Fund (UNFPA);*
- *UNFPA Research. Early marriages and pregnancies, Italian translation by Aidos, Year 2013;*
- *Alberto Sofia, La vergogna del caso Sahar Gul, [The shame of the Sahar Gul case], Giornalettismo, 12.07.2013;*
- *MATRIFOR Report, MATRIFOR Analytical report, Le Onde Onlus, April 2014;*
- *Programme of the Italian Presidency of the European Union, July-December 2014;*
- *To the Human Rights Council, within its Universal Periodic Review, for consideration at the 20th session (27 October to 7 November 2014);*
- *Motion for a European Parliament resolution on the phenomenon of child brides 29.6.2015;*
- *UN: Human Rights Council: First Resolution to Prevent Child, Early and Forced Marriage; 2 July 2015;*
- *Mozioni concernenti iniziative in ambito internazionale in relazione al fenomeno dei matrimoni precoci e forzati di minori [Motions concerning international initiatives in relation to the phenomenon of child, early and forced marriage], of 16 July 2015, signatory Pia Locatelli;*
- *"Mai più spose bambine" Petition, #maipiùsposebambine, Wanda Montanelli, Avaaz.org, 15 September 2013;*
- *Girls Not Brides international report, It takes a movement: reflecting on five years of progress towards ending child marriage". (Year of Publication: 2016);*

...

- *"I am Nujood, age 10 and divorced" by Nujood Ali and Delphine Minoui published on the 22 January 2009 by Michel Lafon, 1 March 2010;*

- *Le spose-bambine derubate del futuro* [Child-brides deprived of their future] – Dossier by Save The Children, *Famiglia Cristiana* [Italian magazine], 05/08/2014;
- *Who is Malala Yousafzai? Nobel Peace Prize 2014*, Public Sphere, 10 October 2014;
- Roberto Vicario, *Recensione Difret Il Coraggio Per Cambiare, L'emancipazione Della Donna, raccontata con coraggio!* [Review of 'Difret' - the Courage to Change, Women's emancipation, told with courage!] *game surf*, 21 January 2015;
- Memory Banda, *A warrior's cry against child marriage*, TEDWomen 2015 ('I will marry when I want'.) *https://www.ted.com*;
- Zeresenay Berhane Mehari 2014, *Difret, from ComboniFem*, Missione Vicenza webdiocesi, March 2015;
- *Young Afghan rapper escaped a forced marriage thanks to her music*, Global Voices, 25 May 2015;
- Sonita Alizadeh. *Brides for Sale*, Antiwarsongs.org, 26 June 2015;
- Girls Not Brides, *New Research Identifies What Works Best To Delay Marriage In Ethiopia And Tanzania*, 18th Aug 2015;
- *On Day of the Girl, join #MyLifeAt15 & tell governments to end child marriage now!* Girls Not Brides, 1 Oct. 2015;
- Joyce Hackel AND Julia Barton, *The Story Of One Girl Who Fought Abduction, And The Lawyers Who Saved Her Life*, Pri's The World, October 22, 2015;
- Valeria Panzeri, *Mariama, 13 anni, era la migliore della scuola, l'hanno venduta per 152,42 euro* [Mariama, 13 years old, she was top of her school, they sold her for 152.42 euro], Urbanpost.it, 18 November 2015;
- Valeria Panzeri, *Speciale Spose bambine* [Child brides special]: *Aisha orfana, malata e secondo lo zio posseduta dal maligno*, [Aisha an orphan, ill and possessed by demons according to her uncle], Urbanpost.it 14 January 2016;
- *Tanzania Wins UN Praise for Anti-FGM Stance*, Daily News (Dar es Salaam), 11 Feb. 2016;
- La Tanzania ottiene l'elogio dell'ONU per le Deliberazioni contro l'infibulazione e I Matrimoni Precoci [Tanzania earns the praise of the UN for its Resolutions against infibulation and early marriage], Onerpo, February 2016;
- Nepal Girl Summit, *His Royal Highness Prince Harry opens the Nepal Girl Summit*, government/news/nepal-girl-summit 23 March 2016, *www.gov.uk*;

- 'Il 'Nepal Girls Summit' Per Un Reale Cambiamento Contro I Matrimoni Precoci E Le Mutilazioni Genitali Femminili, [Nepal Girls Summit' for a Real Change Against Child Marriage and Female Genital Mutilation], Onerpo, 25 March 2016;
- Keep Reading, Reflecting on national strategies to end child marriage: lessons from ..., In Terris, 22 Apr. 2016;
- Paola Amicucci, Kriti, la ragazza indiana che ha salvato 900 bambini dai matrimoni forzati, [Kriti, the Indian girl who has saved 900 children from forced marriage], Corriere della Sera, 20 May 2016;
- Geraldina Colotti, Spose bambine, Erdoğan cede alla piazza, [Geraldina Colotti, child brides, Erdoğan gives in], Il Messaggero, 23.11.2016;
- Ellen Travers (Girls Not Brides) and Meg Greene (Greene Works), New research on child marriage in 2016: what did we learn?, Girls Not Brides, 26th Jan 2017;
- Matilda Branson, Reflecting on national strategies to end child marriage: lessons from 11 countries, Girls Not Brides, 10th Feb 2017;
- Onerpo, matrimoni precoci in Messico [child marriage in Mexico]. La storia di Itzel sposata a 14 anni, [The story of Itzel married at 14], (Girls Not Brides, A day in the life of Itzel, a 15-year-old bride in Mexico 25th Apr. 2017);
- Ellen Travers, Girls Not Brides on Thursday 6th July 2017 (title?
- Abdul Gani, Darrang, Assam Facebook And WhatsApp Are Helping Check Child Marriages In Assam, Huffingtonpost.In, 22 June 2017;
- What if radio could end child marriage? Stories from the DRC - Girls Not Brides, 13 February 2018;
- Mario Consani, Matrimonio combinato dal padre col nipote in Bangladesh: la donna strappa i passaporti, lui chiede il duplicato per il viaggio, [Father arranged marriage with his nephew in Bangladesh: the woman tore up their passports, he asked for duplicates for the trip] Il Giorno, 27 May 2018;
- Malaysian National Che Abdul Karim, 41, Weds 11-Year-Old Thai Girl, 2 July 2018, News From Women;
- The bride's a child? Photographer refuses to take pictures and becomes a hero, Globalist, 10 July 2018;
- Lakshmi Sundaram, Incontro Globale Girls Not Brides 2018, Onerpo, (Ten Takeaways From The Girls Not Brides Global Meeting) July 2018;

- *Martina Di Pirro e Christian Elia, Storia di K., sposa bambina e baby schiava, [K's story, child bride and baby slave], L'Espresso, 27 July 2018;*
- *Debora Attanasio, Negli Stati Uniti sposare una bambina è legale (e nessuno se ne accorge), [It's legal to marry a child in the U.S. (and nobody notices)], Marie Claire, 20/08/2018;*
- *Lakshmi Sundaram, Ten takeaways from the Girls Not Brides Global Meeting - 11th July 2018;*
- *Turchia, fotografo si rifiuta di lavorare al matrimonio perché la sposa aveva 15 anni, [Turkey, photographer refuses to work at a wedding because the bride was 15 years old], Blitz Quotidiano, 12 July 2018;*
- *Pakistan: drivers paint 'studying girl' image on trucks to advocate women's right to education, by newsd, 03rd December 2018; (Pakistan: I conducenti dipingono le immagini di Studentesse sui camion per difendere il diritto all'istruzione delle ragazze, Onerpo, 5 Dec. 2018).*

CONTENTS


# CHAPTER I


## STORIES ABOUT CHILD BRIDES

CHAPTER II


ARE THINGS CHANGING FOR GIRLS?

CHAPTER III

THE PETITIONS, THE APPEALS AND THE WEB IN
AID OF LITTLE GIRLS

## THE INITIATIVES OF THE VARIOUS GOVERNMENTS

CHAPTER IV

OTHER CASES OF ABUSED GIRLS



THE STORIES TOLD ON THE RADIO

NOTES

[1] *Ilaria Sesana, Le spose-bambine derubate del futuro [Child-brides deprived of their future] - Famiglia Cristiana, 05/08/2014;*
[2] *Ibidem;*
[3] *Child marriages in Mexico. The story of Itzel married at 14, Onerpo; A day in the life of Itzel, a 15-year-old, Girls Not Brides, 26 April 2017;*
[4] *"I am Nujood, age 10 and divorced" by Nujood Ali and Delphine Minoui published on the 22 January 2009 by Michel Lafon;*
[5] *Who is Malala Yousafzai? Nobel Peace Prize 2014, Public Sphere, 10 October 2014;*
[6] *Roberto Vicario, Review of "Difret, the Courage to Change", Women's emancipation, told with courage! Game Surf, 21 January 2015;*
[7] *Lakshmi Sundaram, Ten takeaways from the Girls Not Brides Global Meeting - 11 July 2018;*
[8] *Memory Banda, A warrior's cry against child marriage, TEDWomen 2015 ('I will marry when I want'. https://www.ted.com;*
[9] *Letter from Ambassador Sebastiano Cardi, Permanent Representative of Italy to the United Nations in New York, addressed, to Onerpo, 23 November 2016;*
[10] *Chamber of Deputies, Texts on the agenda- meeting no. 463, Thursday 16 July 2015;*
[11] *Ibidem;*
[12] *Chamber of Deputies Resolution 21 July 2014 signed by Locatelli, Zampa, Bergamini, Binetti, Galgano, Gigli, Spadoni, Nicchi, Gebhard, Giorgia Meloni, Bechis, Albanella, Amato, Carocci, Chaouki, Cimbro, Di Gioia, Di Lello, Di Salvo, Fabbri, Fitzgerald Nissoli, Gadda, Gribaudo, Gullo, Iori, Patrizia Maestri, Malpezzi, Marzano, Mongiello, Palma, Pastorelli, Piazzoni, Piccione, Quartapelle Procopio, Rocchi, Sbrollini, Tidei, Tinagli, Venittelli, Ventricelli, Vezzali, Villecco Calipari, Carfagna, Giammanco, Scuvera, Antimo Cesaro, Artini, Baldassarre, Barbanti, Matarrelli, Mucci, Prodani, Rizzetto, Segoni, Turco, Antezza, Labriola, Amoddio, Boldrini, Carnevali;*
[13] *document no. 1-00945, 13 July 2015, signed by Rondini, Fedriga, Allasia, Attaguile, Borghesi, Bossi, Filippo Busin, Caparini, Giancarlo Giorgetti, Grimoldi, Guidesi, Invernizzi, Marcolin, Molteni, Gianluca Pini, Saltamartini, Simonetti);*
[14] *Italian Senate –motion 1-00637, 4 October 2016, Signed by Fedeli, Stefani, Bianconi, Bernini, De Petris, Bonfrisco, Bencini, Gambaro, Repetti, Bisinella, Albano, Amati, Astorre, Bellot, Cantini, Cardinali, Cirinna', Cuomo, D'adda, Dalla Zuanna, Fabbri, Fasiolo, Ferrara Elena, Filippin, Giacobbe, Ginetti, Idem, Lo Giudice, Manassero, Mattesini, Maturani, Munerato, Orru', Padua, Pezzopane, Puglisi, Puppato, Ranucci, Rossi Gianluca, Sangalli, Sollo, Spilabotte, Vaccari, Valdinosi, Sonego, Saggese;*
[15] *Child marriage costs trillions of dollars in the world, Onerpo, 5 Sept. 2018, free partial translation (Rachel Clement, The economic and human costs of child marriage - and what we can do about them, 5th Sep. 2018);*
[16] *Pakistan: drivers paint 'studying girl' image on trucks to advocate women's right to education, by newsd, 03rd December 2018; (Pakistan) (Onerpo translation, 5 December 2018);*

[17] *Maria Sordino, Sonita Alizadeh fights back: "Mai più spose bambine" [No more child brides], 2anews.it, 29-10-2017;*

[18] *Young Afghan rapper escaped a forced marriage thanks to her music, Global Voices, 25 May 2015;*

[19] *Sonita Alizadeh,* Brides for Sale, *www.antiwarsongs.org/canzone.php?lang=en&id=50101, 26 June 2015;*

[20] *Valeria Panzeri, Speciale Spose bambine [Child brides special]: Aisha orfana, malata e posseduta dal maligno, secondo lo zio [Aisha an orphan, ill and possessed by demons according to her uncle], Urban Post, 14 January 2016;*

[21] *Turkey, photographer refuses to work at a wedding because the bride was 15 years old, Blitz Quotidiano, 12 July 2018;*

[22] *"Mai più spose bambine" Petition, #maipiùsposebambine, Wanda Montanelli, Avaaz.org, 15 September 2013;*

[23] *Wanda Montanelli, Matrimoni precoci e forzati in Europa [Child, early and forced marriage in Europe], report of 4 March 2016, Nuova aula del palazzo dei Gruppi parlamentari via di campo marzio 78, Rome. (Amnesty International Conference, Renouncing childhood too soon: child, early and forced marriage, a violation of human rights).*